MICROWAVE COOKING FOR TODAY'S LIVING

PRECAUTIONS TO AVOID POSSIBLE EXPOSURE TO EXCESSIVE MICRO-WAVE ENERGY.

1. Do not attempt to operate this oven with the door open since open-door operation can result in harmful exposure to microwave energy. It is important not to defeat or tamper with the safety interlocks.

2. Do not place any object between the oven front face and the door or allow soil or cleaner residue to accumulate on sealing surfaces.

3. Do not operate the oven if it is damaged. It is particularly important that the oven door close properly and that there is no damage to the:

   (1) door (bent)

   (2) hinges and latches (broken or loosened)

   (3) door seals and sealing surfaces.

4. The oven should not be adjusted or repaired by anyone except properly qualified service personnel.

TABLE OF CONTENTS

Introduction

Recipes

Appendix

Index

INTRODUCTION

1. How Your Microwave Oven Works

Microwaves are a form of energy similar to radio and television waves. Your microwave oven is constructed in such a way as to take advantage of microwave energy. Electricity is converted into microwave energy by the magnetron tube, and microwaves are then sent into the cooking area through openings at the top of the oven. Microwaves reflect off the metal walls of the oven. Since microwaves do not penetrate metal, cooking utensils made of metal are generally not used for cooking in the microwave. Microwave energy can, however, be transmitted through glass, paper, wicker and microwavable cooking dishes. Microwaves do not heat the cookware, though vessels will eventually feel hot from the heat generated by the food. Microwaves are attracted to the moisture in foods and cause the water molecules to vibrate 2,450 million times per second. This is called absorption. As the water molecules vibrate they rub against each other, producing friction. This friction, in turn, causes the food to get hot. If you have trouble imagining how this is possible, just think how hot your hands would get if you rubbed your palms together 2,450 million times per second!

A safe appliance: When the door is opened, the oven automatically stops producing microwaves. By the time microwave energy has been converted into heat in the process of making food hot, the microwaves have completely dissipated.

2. Getting the Best Results From Your Microwave Oven

Keeping an eye on things: The recipes in this book have been formulated with great care, but your success in preparing them depends on how much attention you pay to the food as it cooks. Your microwave oven is equipped with a light that turns on automatically when the oven is in operation. You can see inside the oven and check the progress of your food. Directions given in recipes to "stir", "turn over", etc., should be considered minimum steps recommended for even cooking and speed in the microwave.

Factors affecting cooking time: The cooking times given in the recipes in this book are approximate. Many factors affect cooking times. The temperature of ingredients used in a recipe makes a big difference in the cooking time. For example a cake made with cold butter, milk, and eggs will take longer to bake than one made with ingredients that are at room temperature.

On very cold or very hot days, a great deal of electricity is diverted for heating and cooling. Thus, less electricity is available for your oven, and the food will cook more slowly than usual.

Range of cooking times: Most of the recipes in this book give a range of cooking times. In general, you will find that the food remains undercooked at the lower end of the time range. Personal preferences vary, as do the cooking speeds of different ovens under different conditions. While undercooked food may always be

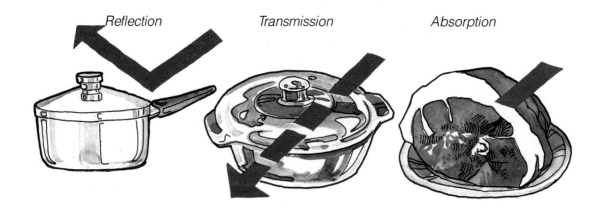

Reflection　　　*Transmission*　　　*Absorption*

cooked a bit more, overcooked food can be ruined. Always add extra time cautiously.

Some of the recipes, particularly those for breads, cakes and meats suggest that food be removed from the oven when it is still slightly undercooked. This is not a mistake. When allowed to stand, the food will continue to cook outside the microwave, as the heat trapped within the outer portions of the food gradually travels inward. As you gain experience in using your microwave, you will become increasingly skillful in estimating both cooking and standing times for various foods.

3. How Characteristics of Foods Affect Microwave Cooking

Quantity: The greater the volume of food, the longer it takes to cook. In general, cooking time is increased by almost 50 percent, when doubling a recipe. Time is reduced by approximately 40 percent when cutting a recipe in half.

Density: Light, porous food such as cakes and breads cook more quickly than heavy, dense food such as roasts, potatoes and casseroles.

Height: Whether conventional or microwave cooking methods are used, areas of food close to the energy source may need to be turned over or shielded for even cooking.

Shape and Size: For more even cooking results, choose food pieces that are similar in size and shape. Arrange small, thin pieces toward the center of the dish and thicker pieces toward the outside of the dish.

Sugar, Fat and Salt: Food with high sugar, fat and salt content cooks faster than food low in these elements.

4. Special Techniques in Microwave Cooking

Browning: Meat and poultry with high fat content that are cooked 10 to 15 minutes or longer, will brown lightly. Food that is cooked for a shorter period of time, may be brushed with a browning agent to achieve an appealing color. The most commonly used browning sauces are Worcestershire sauce, soy sauce and barbecue sauce.

Covering: A cover traps heat and steam causing the food to cook more quickly. You may either use a lid or plastic wrap with a corner folded back to vent the excess steam. Recipes calling for covered microwavable casseroles use the glass casserole lids to help retain the steam, however, the lids can become hot during cooking, so handle carefully. Waxed paper effectively prevents food from spattering in the oven and helps food retain some heat. Sandwiches and many other foods can be wrapped in paper towels to absorb extra moisture.

Spacing: Individual foods such as baked potatoes, cupcakes and hors d'oeuvres will cook more evenly if placed in the oven at least an inch apart, preferably in a circular pattern.

Stirring: Stirring is an important microwaving technique. Microwaved foods are stirred in order to blend flavors and redistribute heat. Always stir from the outside toward the inside, since food at the outside of the dish heats first.

Turning Over: Larger sized food such as roasts and whole poultry should be turned over so that the top and bottom will cook evenly. It is also a good idea to turn over chicken pieces and chops.

Arrangement: Since dense foods cook more slowly in the microwave, it makes sense to place thicker portions of meat, poultry, fish and vegetables to the outer edge of the baking dish. This way, thicker portions will receive the most microwave energy and the food will cook evenly. Also, arrange food in a single layer rather than stacking to permit more even cooking.

Testing for Doneness: Because foods cook so quickly in a microwave oven, it is necessary to test for doneness frequently. Check recipes for specific visual doneness information.

Standing Time: Food is often allowed to stand for 2 to 15 minutes after being removed from the microwave oven. Usually the food is covered during standing time to retain heat. Most foods are removed from the oven while still slightly undercooked, and finish cooking during standing time. The internal temperature of food will rise about 10°F. during standing time.

Shielding: Strips of aluminum foil, which block microwaves, are sometimes placed over the corners or edges of square and rectangular shaped dishes to prevent those portions from overcooking. Irregular food shapes such as poultry legs and wings tips can be shielded with foil to keep them from overcooking. Keep foil at least one inch away from the oven walls.

Piercing: To prevent bursting, food enclosed in a shell, skin or membrane must be pierced prior to cooking. Such foods include both the yolks and whites of eggs, hot dogs, clams, oysters and many whole vegetables, such as potatoes and squash.

5. Microwave-Safe Utensils

Never use metal or metal-trimmed utensils in your microwave oven. Microwaves cannot penetrate metal. They will bounce off any metal object in the oven and cause "arcing", which resembles lightning. Most heat-resistant, non-metallic cooking utensils are safe for use in your microwave oven. However, some may contain materials that render them unsuitable for microwave cooking. If you have any doubts about a particular utensil, there's a simple way to find out if it can be used in your microwave oven.

Testing Utensils for Microwave Use: Place the utensil in question next to a one cup glass measuring cup filled with water in the microwave. Cook 1 minute at Power Control 10. If the water is warm and the utensil remains cool, the utensil is microwavable. However, if the utensil becomes warm, microwaves are being absorbed by the utensil and it should not be used in the microwave oven.

You probably have many items on hand in your kitchen right now that can be used as cooking equipment in your microwave oven. Read through the following checklist.

1. Dinner Plates: Many kinds of tableware are microwavable. If in doubt, consult the manufacturer's literature or perform the utensil test for microwave use.

2. Glassware: Some glassware that is heat-resistant is microwavable. This would include most brands of oven-tempered glass cookware. Do not, however, use delicate tumblers, wine glasses, etc. in the oven, as they may possibly shatter.

3. Paper: Paper plates and containers without wax coatings are convenient and safe to use in your microwave oven for short cooking times. Paper towels are also very useful for absorbing moisture and grease. In general, use white paper, as some dyes may separate.

4. Plastic Storage Containers: These can be used to hold foods that are to be quickly reheated. However, they should not be used to heat foods that will need considerable time in the oven, as hot foods will eventually warp or melt the containers.

5. Cooking Bags: Cooking bags are microwavable. Make sure to make a slit in the bag so that steam can escape. Substitute string or microwavable closure for metal twist ties.

6. Plastic Microwave Cookware: A variety of cookware is available. Certain specialty items such as plastic ring molds, muffin pans, etc. are convenient. Check the manufacturer's instructions.

7. Pottery, Stoneware and Ceramic: Containers made of these materials are usually safe for use in your microwave. They should be checked by using the dish test.

8. Wicker, Straw and Wood: All of these materials are safe for brief use in your microwave oven. Remove any metal fittings.

9. Metal Utensils: Metal utensils and utensils with metal straps, clips or screws should not be placed in your microwave while it is in operation. Use wooden skewers, which are available at most cookware shops.

10. Browning Skillets: Browning skillets or grills are useful to provide extra surface browning of meats such as steaks and hamburgers. They heat to a very high temperature and should be handled with great care. Follow the manufacturer's guidelines for directions and proper use.

Do not use these utensils

6. Some Microwaving Tips

Boiling Water: Place 1 cup of water in a 2-cup glass measuring cup and cook uncovered 2½ to 3 minutes at Power Control 10, or until boiling.

Instant Coffee: Place 6 ounces of water in a microwavable cup or mug. Cook uncovered 1½ to 2 minutes at Power Control 10, or until hot. Stir in coffee crystals.

Hot Cocoa: Place 1 or 2 teaspoons each of cocoa powder and sugar in an 8-ounce mug. Gradually add 6 ounces of milk stirring to blend. Cook uncovered 1 to 2 minutes at Power Control 8, or until hot, stirring once.

Heating Syrup or Honey: Place in a glass pitcher and cook uncovered at Power Control 10 until warm; stir once. One cup syrup or honey will take 2 to 3 minutes, or until warm.

Melting Butter or Margarine: Place butter or margarine in a custard cup or glass measuring cup. Cook uncovered at Power Control 10 until melted.

Softening Butter, Margarine or Cream Cheese: Unwrap and place on a serving plate. Cook uncovered at Power Control 1 checking at 20 second intervals.

Melting Chocolate Squares and Chocolate Pieces: Place in a custard cup or glass bowl and cook uncovered at Power Control 7. One square of unsweetened chocolate or 1 cup of chocolate pieces will take about 2 to 3 minutes. Two squares of unsweetened chocolate or 2 cups of chocolate pieces will take 4 to 6 minutes. Stir until smooth.

Melting Caramels: Combine 1 14 ounce package of caramels and 2 tablespoons of water in a 4-cup glass measuring cup. Cook uncovered 3 to 4 minutes at Power Control 7, or until melted, stirring every minute.

Toasting Almonds: Place sliced or slivered almonds in a shallow baking dish and add 1 teaspoon of butter or margarine per ½ cup of nuts. Cook uncovered 3 to 4 minutes at Power Control 10, or until light brown, stirring every minute.

Toasting Coconut: Place unsweetened, flaked or grated coconut in a 9-inch glass pie plate. Cook uncovered 3 to 4 minutes at Power Control 7, or until light brown. Stir every minute.

Freshening Up Stale Chips and Pretzels: Place chips or pretzels in a napkin-lined wicker basket. Cook uncovered about 30 seconds per cup at Power Control 10, or until snacks feel warm. Let stand a few minutes to cool before serving.

Warming Bread and Rolls: Wrap in a napkin or place in a napkin-lined wicker basket. Cook uncovered 30 seconds to 1 minute at Power Control 8, or until bread or rolls feel warm.

Cooking Bacon: Place bacon slices on a double thickness of paper towel on a paper plate and cover with a paper towel. Cook uncovered 1 to 1½ minutes per slice at Power Control 10, or until crisp. If you wish to save the drippings, cook bacon on a rack placed inside a microwavable baking dish.

7. Microwave Power Controls

Your microwave oven is equipped with ten power levels (11 steps including 0) to give you maximum flexibility and control over cooking. When your cooking program is completed, a beeper automatically sounds. The table below will give you some idea of which foods are prepared at each of the various power levels.

MICROWAVE POWER CONTROL CHART

Power Control	Examples	Microwave Output Power*
1	• Softening cream cheese. • Keeping casseroles and main dishes warm.	90
2	• Softening chocolate. • Heating breads, rolls, pancakes, tacos, tortillas, French toast. • Clarifying butter. • Taking the chill out of fruit. • Heating small amounts of food.	160
3	• Thawing meat, poultry and seafood. • Finish cooking casseroles, stews, and some sauces. • Cooking small quantities of most food.	225
4	• Cooking pork roast, corned beef, stew meat, pork chops, loin roast. • Reheat frozen convenience foods. • Cooking less tender cuts of meat in liquid or slow cooking dishes.	285
5	• Cooking soups after bringing to a boil. • Cooking baked custards. • Cooking whole chicken, turkey, spare ribs, duckling, rib roast, sirloin roast, lamb roast, ham.	350
6	• Cooking pasta.	400
7	• Cooking cheese dishes, veal. • Cooking cakes, muffins, brownies, cupcakes, convenience baking mixes. • Cooking quick breads and cereal products.	490
8	• Reheating precooked or prepared food. • Heating sandwiches. • Cooking scrambled eggs.	500
9	• Cooking onions, celery and green peppers. • Reheating meat slices.	560
HI (Max Power)	• Cooking fish, vegetables and most casseroles. • Boiling water. • Thickening some sauces.	650

* Approximate watts as measured by 2-liter method.

APPETIZERS

Curried Chicken Balls

APPETIZERS

Cooking Appetizers: Tips and Techniques

Appetizers such as meatballs and dips can be prepared ahead of time. Reheat in the microwave and they are ready for guests in no time.

- Arrange individual appetizers in a circle for even cooking.
- Stir dips to distribute heat and shorten cooking time.
- Crisp crackers such as melba toast, shredded wheat and crisp rye crackers are the best for microwave use. Wait until party time to add the spreads. A paper towel placed under crackers while cooking in the microwave helps absorb extra moisture.
- Cover foods to retain moisture. Cook uncovered to ensure crispness.
- Avoid overcooking by using the minimum recommended time. Add more time if necessary, only after checking.
- Appetizers with a crisp coating or puff pastry crust are best done in a conventional oven with dry heat.
- Breaded products can be warmed in the microwave but will not come out crisp.

Nachos

15 tortilla chips
3 tablespoons jalapeno bean dip
½ cup shredded Cheddar cheese

1. Spread each tortilla chip with bean dip; top with cheese. Place chips on a paper plate.
2. Cook uncovered 1 to 1½ minutes at Power Control 7 or until cheese is melted.

Makes 15 appetizers.

Stuffed Mushrooms

8 large mushrooms (½ pound)
⅓ cup finely chopped green onion
3 tablespoons butter or margarine
2 tablespoons dried bread crumbs
½ tablespoon dried parsley flakes

1. Clean mushrooms; remove and chop stems. Reserve mushroom caps and ⅓ cup chopped stems.
2. Place reserved chopped mushroom stems, green onion and butter in a 1-quart microwavable casserole. Cook uncovered 3 to 4 minutes at Power Control 10 or until onion is tender; stir twice. Stir in bread crumbs and parsley flakes
3. Stuff each mushroom cap with bread crumb mixture. Arrange stuffed mushrooms in a circle on a paper towel-lined paper plate. Cover with waxed paper and cook 1½ to 2 minutes at Power Control 10 until hot.

Makes 8 appetizers.

12

Curried Chicken Balls

½ cup finely chopped, cooked chicken
1 tablespoon chopped raisins
1 tablespoon dried bread crumbs
1 teaspoon dried onion flakes
1 tablespoon mayonnaise
½ teaspoon lemon juice
¼ teaspoon curry powder
1 egg, slightly beaten
½ cup dried bread crumbs
Chutney mayonnaise

1. Combine ingredients, except egg, ½ cup bread crumbs and chutney mayonnaise. Shape into 8 balls.
2. Dip balls into beaten egg and roll in reserved crumbs. Arrange balls in a circle on paper plate. Cook uncovered 1½ to 2 minutes at Power Control 10 or until heated through. Serve with chutney mayonnaise.

Makes 8 appetizers.

Sweet and Sour Tuna Crackers

1 can (3¼ ounces) tuna, drained and flaked
1 package (3 ounces) cream cheese, softened
2 tablespoons crushed pineapple, drained
½ tablespoon white vinegar
⅛ teaspoon curry powder
24 crackers or melba toast rounds

1. Combine ingredients, except crackers in a mixing bowl; blend thoroughly.
2. Spread mixture on crackers. Arrange 8 crackers in a circle on a paper plate. Cook uncovered 30 to 40 seconds at Power Control 10 or until tuna mixture bubbles. Repeat with remaining crackers.

Makes 24 appetizers.

Chili Con Queso Dip

1 pound pasteurized process cheese spread, cut into cubes
1 can (15 ounces) chili with beans
1 can (10 ounces) whole tomatoes and green chilies, chopped
Tortilla chips or crisp raw vegetables

1. Combine ingredients in a 1½-quart covered microwavable casserole. Cook covered 9 to 10 minutes at Power Control 7 or until heated through; stir once halfway through cooking.
2. Stir well. Let stand covered 5 minutes. Serve with tortilla chips or crisp raw vegetables.

Makes about 4 cups.

SAUCES & DESSERT TOPPINGS

Spaghetti Sauce

SAUCES & DESSERT TOPPINGS

Once you begin cooking sauces and toppings in the microwave, you'll never go back to cooking them conventionally. Measure, mix and cook the ingredients in a glass measuring cup or microwavable serving dish or casserole.

Cooking Sauces: Tips and Techniques

- Use a microwavable casserole or glass measuring cup that is at least two or three times the volume of the sauce.
- Sauces made with cornstarch thicken more rapidly than those thickened with flour.
- Sauces made with cornstarch or flour are usually cooked uncovered so they may be stirred 2 to 3 times during cooking for a smooth consistency.
- To adapt a conventional sauce or gravy recipe, reduce the amount of liquid slightly.

White Sauce

2 tablespoons butter or margarine
2 tablespoons flour
¼ teaspoon salt
⅛ teaspoon ground white pepper (optional)
1 cup milk

1. Place butter in a 1-quart microwavable casserole. Cook uncovered 30 to 45 seconds at Power Control 10 or until melted. Stir in flour, salt and pepper making a smooth paste. Gradually add milk; blend thoroughly.
2. Cook uncovered 4 to 5 minutes at Power Control 7 or until sauce is thickened and bubbly, stir occasionally.

Makes 1 cup.

Variations

Cheese Sauce: Stir ½ to ¾ cup shredded cheese (Cheddar, Swiss, Parmesan, or combination of cheeses) into finished sauce. Cook uncovered 1 to 1½ minutes at Power Control 6 or until cheese is melted.
Curry Sauce: Stir 1 to 2 teaspoons curry powder into flour. Continue as directed.
Mustard Sauce: Stir 2 to 3 tablespoons prepared mustard into finished sauce. Season with ⅛ teaspoon Worcestershire sauce.

Basic Brown Sauce

¼ cup finely chopped onion
¼ cup butter or margarine or meat drippings
3 tablespoons flour
1 can (10½ ounces) condensed beef broth
⅓ cup water
⅛ teaspoon ground black pepper
⅛ teaspoon thyme leaves

1. Combine onion and butter in a 1-quart microwavable casserole. Cook covered 2 to 3 minutes at Power Control 10 or until onion is tender.
2. Stir flour into onion mixture. Gradually add beef broth and water, stir until smooth. Add remaining ingredients. Cook uncovered 3 to 4 minutes at Power Control 10 or until sauce is thickened; stir twice.

Makes about 1⅔ cups.

Spaghetti Sauce

½ cup finely chopped onion
1 clove garlic, pressed or finely chopped
2 tablespoons olive oil
1 can (15 ounces) tomato sauce
1½ teaspoons dried basil leaves
1½ teaspoons dried oregano leaves
¼ teaspoon ground black pepper

1. Combine onion, garlic and oil in a 1-quart microwavable casserole. Cook uncovered 2 to 3 minutes at Power Control 10 or until onion is tender.
2. Add remaining ingredients. Cook covered 3 minutes at Power Control 10 and then 10 minutes at Power Control 5; stir twice.

Makes about 1¾ cups.

Chocolate Sauce

¼ cup sugar
1 tablespoon cocoa
1 teaspoon flour
Dash of salt
2 tablespoons milk
2 teaspoons butter or margarine
2 teaspoons light corn syrup
¼ teaspoon vanilla extract

1. Combine dry ingredients in a 1-quart glass measuring cup; stir in milk. Add butter and corn syrup.
2. Cook uncovered 1½ to 2½ minutes at Power Control 10 or until sauce is thickened and smooth; stir twice. Stir in vanilla extract.

Makes ½ cup.

Vanilla Sauce

⅓ cup sugar
2 tablespoons cornstarch
1½ cups milk, divided
2 tablespoons butter or margarine, cut into small pieces
1 tablespoon vanilla extract

1. Combine sugar and cornstarch in a 1-quart glass measuring cup. Whisk in enough milk to make a smooth paste. Stir in remaining milk. Cook uncovered 6 to 7 minutes at Power Control 7 or until sauce is thickened; stir twice.
2. Stir in butter and vanilla extract. Serve over cake or fruit.

Makes about 1¾ cups.

Cherry Sauce with Brandy

½ cup sugar
2 tablespoons cornstarch
1 can (16 ounces) pitted cherries in heavy syrup
1 tablespoon lemon juice
¼ cup brandy

1. Combine sugar and cornstarch in a 1-quart glass measuring cup. Gradually add cherries and lemon juice; stir to blend. Cover with plastic wrap; vent.
2. Cook covered 5 to 6 minutes at Power Control 10 or until sauce is hot and thickened; stir once. Stir in brandy. Serve warm over ice cream or cake.

Makes about 2½ cups.

SOUPS

Bouillabaisse

SOUPS

Soups cook quickly in a microwavable bowl or casserole for convenient microwave-to-table serving. They require very little attention and taste like they have been simmered all day. Clean-up is a breeze.

Cooking Soups: Tips & Techniques

- Cook soups in a microwavable dish which holds double the volume of the recipe ingredients to prevent boil-over, especially if cream or milk is used in the soup.
- Generally, microwaved soups are covered with either plastic wrap, vented or a microwavable lid.
- Stirring occasionally will help blend flavors, distribute the heat evenly and may even shorten cooking time.
- When converting a conventional soup recipe to microwave, reduce liquid, salt and strong seasonings.

Bouillabaisse

12 to 16	medium clams in shells
2	small lobster tails
2	pounds perch fillets
1½	cups chopped onion
1	clove garlic, pressed or finely chopped
¼	cup vegetable oil
1	can (16 ounces) tomatoes, undrained
1	cup water
¼	cup chopped parsley
1	bay leaf
2	teaspoons dried basil
½	teaspoon salt
¼	teaspoon ground black pepper

1. Wash clams thoroughly. Split lobster tails in half lengthwise, then cut each length into 1-inch chunks. Cut fish fillets into 1-inch chunks. Set aside.
2. Combine onion, garlic and oil in a 4-quart microwavable casserole. Cook uncovered 4 to 5 minutes at Power Control 10 or until tender; stir once. Add remaining ingredients, except clams, lobster and fish. Cook covered 10 minutes at Power Control 10; stir twice.
3. Add clams, lobster and fish. Cook covered 7 to 8 minutes at Power Control 10 or until lobster and fish are opaque and clam shells are open; stir twice. Let stand covered 5 minutes. Remove bay leaf before serving.

Makes 6 servings.

Consommé Madrilene

1	can (10½ ounces) condensed consommé
⅓	cup tomato juice
⅓	cup water
2	tablespoons dry sherry
½	teaspoon lemon juice
	Dairy sour cream (optional)
	Chopped parsley (optional)

1. Combine ingredients in a 1-quart glass measuring cup.
2. Cook uncovered 5 to 6 minutes at Power Control 7 or until hot; stir once. Garnish with sour cream and parsley.

Makes 2 servings.

Vegetable Soup

2 cups chicken broth
2 stalks celery, thinly sliced
1 medium potato, cut into ½-inch cubes
1 small onion, sliced
1 carrot, thinly sliced
1 tablespoon finely chopped parsley
½ teaspoon dried basil leaves
¼ teaspoon salt
1 small tomato, peeled, seeded and chopped
1 cup torn spinach leaves
½ cup frozen cut green beans, thawed
½ cup frozen peas, thawed
½ cup frozen caulifower, thawed and chopped

1. Combine broth, celery, potato, onion, carrot, parsley, basil and salt in a 3-quart microwavable casserole. Cook covered 15 minutes at Power Control 10.
2. Add remaining ingredients. Cook covered 10 to 15 minutes at Power Control 10 or until vegetables are tender.

Makes 3 to 4 servings.

Onion Soup

1 cup thinly sliced onions
2 tablespoons butter or margarine
1 can (10½ ounces) condensed beef broth
1 slice of toasted French bread
½ cup shredded Swiss cheese
2 tablespoons grated Parmesan cheese

1. Combine onions and butter in a 1-quart microwavable casserole. Cook uncovered 3 to 4 minutes at Power Control 10 or until onions are soft; stir twice.
2. Add beef broth. Cook uncovered 2½ to 3½ minutes at Power Control 10 or until hot; stir once after 2 minutes.
3. Ladle into large soup bowl. Cover with bread slice and sprinkle with cheeses. Cook uncovered 1 to 1½ minutes at Power Control 10 or until cheese is melted.

Makes 1 serving.

Minestrone

4 tablespoons olive oil
1 small onion, thinly sliced
1 small carrot, thinly sliced
1 clove garlic, minced
2 cups chicken broth
2 cups water
⅓ cup uncooked spaghetti, broken into small pieces
1 teaspoon oregano leaves
1 teaspoon dried parsley flakes
½ teaspoon salt
¼ teaspoon ground black pepper
1 can (16 ounces) tomatoes, coarsely chopped
1 can (16 ounces) kidney beans, drained
½ cup frozen peas, thawed

1. Combine oil, onion, carrot and garlic in a 3-quart microwavable casserole. Cook covered 5 to 6 minutes at Power Control 10 or until vegetables are tender; stir once.
2. Add broth, water, spaghetti, oregano, parsley, salt and pepper. Cook covered 8 minutes at Power Control 10; stir once.
3. Add tomatoes, kidney beans and peas. Cook covered 8 to 10 minutes at Power Control 5 or until vegetables are tender; stir twice.

Makes 4 servings.

MEAT

Stuffed Flank Steak

MEAT

Now with the help of your microwave, you can serve up twice the meal in half the time. Best of all, you don't have to remember to take the meat out of the freezer in the morning for an evening meal. Defrosting techniques and fast cooking eliminate all these meal-planning roadblocks.

Most meats cook in less time than it takes conventionally. They stay juicy because they are not exposed to hot dry air. For the same reason, the outside usually does not become as dry and crisp as when conventionally roasted.

Defrosting Meat: Tips & Techniques

- For best results, remove meat from original paper or plastic closed package (wrapper). Otherwise, the wrap will hold steam and juice close to the foods which can cause the outer surface of the foods to cook.
- Place meat on microwavable roast rack.
- Defrost meat only as long as necessary. Separate items like chops, hot dogs and bacon as soon as possible.
- Remove and continue to defrost remaining pieces.
- Shield with foil any thin, uneven or warm areas of meat in the middle of the defrosting cycle.
- Whole pieces of meat are ready for standing time as soon as a fork can be pushed into the center of the meat using moderate pressure. The center will still be icy.
  Allow to stand until completely thawed.

MEAT DEFROSTING TABLE

Cut and Weight	Power Control	Time (per pound)	Standing Time	Directions
BEEF Ground beef (1 lb.)	3	4-5 min.	5 min.	Turn over once.* Remove thawed portions with fork. Return remainder to oven and defrost. (The best way to freeze ground beef is in a doughnut shape.)
Pot roast chuck (Under 4 lbs.)	3	3-5 min.	10 min.	Turn over once.*
Rib roast, rolled (3 to 4 lbs.)	3	6-8 min.	30-45 min.	Turn over once.*
Rump roast (3 to 4 lbs.)	3	5-7 min.	30 min.	Turn over once.*
Round steak	3	4-5 min.	5-10 min.	Turn over once.*
Flank steak	3	4-5 min.	5-10 min.	Turn over once.*
Sirloin steak (½ inch thick)	3	4-5 min.	5-10 min.	Turn over once.*
Tenderloin steak	3	4-5 min.	10 min.	Turn over once.*
Stew beef (2 lbs.)	3	3-5 min.	10 min.	Turn over once.* Separate.

* Turning, stirring or shielding should be done in the middle of the defrosting cycle.

MEAT DEFROSTING TABLE (continued)

Cut and Weight	Power Control	Time (per pound)	Standing Time	Directions
LAMB Cubes for stew	3	7-8 min.	5 min.	Turn over once.* Separate.
Ground lamb (Under 4 lbs.)	3	3-5 min.	5 min.	Turn over once.*
Chops (1 inch thick)	3	5-7 min.	15 min.	Turn over once.*
PORK Chops (½ inch thick)	3	4-6 min.	5-10 min.	Separate chops halfway through defrosting time.
Spareribs. Country-style ribs (2 to 3 lbs.)	3	5-7 min.	10 min.	Turn over once.*
Roast (Under 4 lbs.)	3	4-5 min.	20-30 min.	Turn over once.*
Bacon (1 lb.)	3	2-3 min.	5 min.	Defrost until strips separate.
Sausage, bulk (1 lb.)	3	2-3 min.	5 min.	Turn over once.* Remove thawed portions with fork. Return remainder to oven and defrost.
Sausage, links, (1 lb.)	3	3-5 min.	5 min.	Turn over once.* Defrost until pieces can be separated.
Hot dogs (1 lb.)	3	5-6 min.	5 min.	Turn over once.* Separate.
Chops (½ inch thick.)	3	4-6 min.	20 min.	Turn over once.* Separate chops and continue defrosting.

* Turning, stirring or shielding should be done in the middle of the defrosting cycle.

Cooking Meat: Tips & Techniques

- Defrost meat completely before cooking.
- Trim off excess fat.
- Place meat fat side down on microwavable roast rack.
- Turn over and rotate halfway through cooking to insure even cooking.
- Arrange meat so thicker portions are toward outside of dish.
- Drain juices as they accumulate to minimize spattering and avoid undercooking bottom of meat.
- Shield thin or bony portions with strips of foil to prevent overcooking. Keep foil at least one inch from oven walls and do not cover more than one-third of the meat with foil at any one time.
- Cover meat with waxed paper to prevent spattering.
- Let meat stand covered with foil 10 to 15 minutes after removing from microwave. Internal temperature of meat may rise 5°F. to 10°F. during standing time.
- Use oven cooking bags for less tender cuts of meat.

MEAT COOKING TABLE

Meat	Power Control	Cooking Time	Special Instructions
BEEF Corned beef (3 lbs.)	(Stage 1), 10 then (Stage 2), 3	15 minutes then 45-50 minutes per pound	Place corned beef in 3-quart microwavable casserole. Pour 1 cup water and desired seasonings over corned beef. Cook covered. Turn over beef twice during cooking. Shield thinner ends with foil. Cook until fork-tender. Let stand covered 15 minutes. Thinly slice beef diagonally across grain.
Cubes for stew (2 lbs., 1-inch cubes)	(Stage 1) 10 then (Stage 2) 3	10 minutes 35 minutes per pound	Place cubes in 2½-quart microwavable casserole. Pour 1 cup water or broth over cubes. Cook covered. Stir cubes halfway through cooking. Cook until fork-tender. Let stand covered 10 minutes.
Ground beef (1 lb.)	10	4½-6 minutes	Crumble beef and place in microwavable sieve or colander. Place sieve in bowl to collect drippings. Cover with waxed paper. Stir after 3 minutes to break meat apart. After cooking let stand covered 2 minutes. If meat is still pink, cover and cook 1 more minute.
Hamburgers, Fresh or defrosted frozen (4 oz, each) 1 patty 2 patties 4 patties	10	 1-1½ minutes 1½-2½ minutes 3-4½ minutes	Form patties with depression in center of each. Place on microwavable roast rack. Brush with browning agent, if desired. Cover with waxed paper. Turn over halfway through cooking. Let stand covered 1 minute.

MEAT COOKING TABLE (continued)

Meat	Power Control	Cooking Time	Special Instructions
Pot roast (3-4 lbs.)	(Stage 1), 10 then (Stage 2), 3	15 minutes then 40-45 minutes per pound	Place roast in large cooking bag; place in microwavable dish. Add desired seasonings and 1 cup liquid over roast. Close bag loosely with microwavable closure or string. Carefully turn over meat after 45 minutes. Continue cooking until fork-tender. Let stand covered 10 minutes.
Rib roast, rolled (3-4 lbs.)	5	10-12 minutes per pound RARE (135°F) 12-14 minutes per pound MEDIUM (155°F) 13-15 minutes per pound WELL (165°F)	Place roast fat side down on microwavable roast rack. Add desired seasonings and cover with waxed paper. Turn over meat halfway through cooking and shield if necessary. If using probe, insert in center of roast during last half of cooking. Remove roast from microwave when desired temperature is reached. Let stand covered with foil 15 minutes. (Temperature may rise about 10°F).
Rump roast, rolled (3-4 lbs.)	3	18-20 minutes per pound RARE (135°F) 19-20 minutes per pound MEDIUM (155°F)	Place roast fat side down on microwavable roast rack. Add desired seasonings and cover with waxed paper. Turn over meat halfway through cooking and shield if necessary. If using probe, insert in center of roast during last half of cooking. Let stand covered with foil 15 minutes. Remove roast from microwave when desired temperature is reached. (Temperature may rise about 10°F).
Sirloin tip roast (3-4 lbs.)	5	10-12 minutes per pound RARE (135°F) 13-15 minutes per pound MEDIUM (155°F)	Place roast fat side down on microwavable roast rack. Add desired seasonings and cover with waxed paper. Turn over meat halfway through cooking and shield if necessary. If using probe insert in center of roast during last half of cooking. Remove roast from microwave when desired temperature is reached. Let stand covered with foil 15 minutes. (Temperature may rise about 10°F).
Veal cutlets, (about 1 lb.) 4 pieces	7	7-9 minutes per pound	Place cutlets in bottom of oiled microwavable baking dish. Add desired seasonings and cover with waxed paper. Turn over and rearrange cutlets halfway through cooking. Let stand covered 2 minutes. Drain on paper towel.
LAMB Lamb roast, rolled, boneless (3-4 lbs.)	5	14-15 minutes per pound RARE (135°F) 17-18 minutes per pound MEDIUM (145°F) 19-20 minutes per pound WELL (155°F)	Place roast fat side up on microwavable roast rack. Brush lamb with marinade or desired seasonings such as rosemary, thyme or marjoram. Cover with waxed paper. Turn over roast after 15 minutes, and again after 30 minutes. Shield if necessary. If using probe, insert in center of roast for last part of cooking. Remove roast from microwave when desired temperature is reached. Let stand covered with foil 15 minutes. (Temperature may rise about 10°F).
Cubes for stew (2 lbs.) 1-inch cubes	(Stage 1) 10 then (Stage 2) 3	10 minutes 35 minutes per pound	Place cubes in 2-quart microwavable casserole. Add desired seasonings such as rosemary, thyme and marjoram and 1 cup water. Cook covered. Stir cubes twice during cooking. Cook until fork-tender. Let stand covered 15 minutes.

MEAT COOKING TABLE (continued)

Meat	Power Control	Cooking Time	Special Instructions
PORK			

Bacon slices
  2 slices
 	
  4 slices
 	
  6 slices
	10	
		1½-2 minutes
		
		3-4 minutes
		
		4½-5½ minutes
			Place bacon slices on microwavable roast rack. Cover with paper towels. After cooking let stand 1 minute.

Canadian bacon
  2 slices
 	
  4 slices
 	
  6 slices
	10	
		30-45 seconds
		
		1-1½ minutes
		
		1-2 minutes
			Place meat on microwavable roast rack. Cover loosely with waxed paper. After cooking let stand 1 minute.

Chops
  (5-7 oz. each)
 	
  2 chops
 	
  4 chops
	3	
		
		20-21 minutes per pound
		
		17-18 minutes per pound (165°F)
			Place chops in microwavable baking dish. Add desired seasonings and cover with plastic wrap; vent. Cook until no longer pink or until internal temperature reaches 170°F. Turn over chops halfway through cooking. Let stand covered 5 minutes. (Temperature may rise about 10°F.)

Ham, boneless
  fully cooked
  2 lbs.
 	
  5 lbs.
	5	10-15 minutes per pound	Place ham on microwavable roast rack. Cover with waxed paper. Turn over ham halfway through cooking. Cook until internal temperature reaches 120°F. Let stand covered 10 minutes.

Ham, center slice (1 lb.)	7	5-6 minutes	Place slices on microwavable roast rack. Cover with plastic wrap; vent. Let stand covered 1 minute.

Hot dogs
  1
 	
  2
 	
  4
	10	
		30-45 seconds
		
		45-60 seconds
		
		1-2 minutes
			Pierce hot dogs and place on microwavable roast rack. Cover with waxed paper. If in bun, wrap in paper towel or paper napkin to absorb moisture. After cooking, let stand 1 minute.

Loin Roast,
  rolled, boneless
  (3½-4½ lbs.)
	3	19-20 minutes per pound (165°F)	Place roast in cooking bag in microwavable dish. Add seasonings and browning agent if desired. Close bag loosely with microwavable closure or string. Turn over roast halfway through cooking. After cooking let stand in bag 15 minutes. (Temperature may rise about 10°F.) Internal temperature of pork should reach 170°F before serving.

Sausage links,
  Fresh or Frozen,
  defrosted
  (1-2 oz. each)
  2 links
 	
  4 links
 	
  6 links
 	
  10 links
  (8 oz. pkg)
	10	
		
		45-60 seconds
		
		1-1½ minutes
		
		1½-2 minutes
		
		1¾-2 minutes
			Pierce links and place on microwavable roast rack. Cover with waxed paper or paper towel. After cooking let stand covered 1 minute.

MEAT COOKING TABLE (continued)

Meat	Power Control	Cooking Time	Special Instructions
Sausage patties, Fresh (2 oz. each)	10		Place sausage patties in a circle on microwavable roast rack. Brush with browning agent if desired. Cover with waxed paper. Turn patties over halfway through cooking. After cooking let stand 2 minutes.
2 patties		1½-2 minutes	
4 patties		2½-3½ minutes	
8 patties		4½-5½ minutes	
Spareribs (2½-3½ lbs.)	5	25-30 minutes per pound (165°F)	Place ribs, cut into serving size pieces, bone side down in large cooking bag. Place bag in 3-quart microwavable casserole. Add 1 cup water to bag. Close bag loosely with microwavable closure or string. Turn over ribs, rearranging carefully, halfway through cooking. Cook until meat is fork-tender. Carefully remove ribs.
	then 5 (if desired)	10 minutes (if desired)	If desired, brush sauce over ribs. Cook covered with waxed paper. Let stand covered 10 minutes. (Temperature may rise about 10°F).*
			* Internal temperature of pork should reach 170°F before serving.

Stuffed Flank Steak

1 cup finely chopped onion
1 clove garlic, minced
¼ cup butter or margarine
1 package (10 ounces) frozen chopped spinach, thawed and well drained
¼ teaspoon ground thyme
¼ teaspoon ground black pepper
1 beef flank steak (about 1½ pounds)
1 cup beef broth
1 can (10¾ ounces) condensed cream of mushroom soup
¼ cup white wine (optional)

1. Combine onion, garlic and butter in a 2-quart microwavable casserole. Cook uncovered 5½ to 6½ minutes at Power Control 10 or until onion is tender; stir once. Add spinach, thyme and pepper. Cook covered 3½ minutes at Power Control 10. Stir once.
2. Pound flank steak with mallet to flatten. Spread spinach mixture on steak and roll up jellyroll-fashion starting from the long edge. Tie with string. Place in 2-quart microwavable casserole.
3. Combine remaining ingredients and pour over steak. Cook covered 9 minutes at Power Control 10. Turn steak over. Cook covered 45 to 50 minutes per pound at Power Control 3 or until tender; turn steak over twice during cooking. Let stand covered 10 minutes.

Makes 4 servings.

Cheesy Meatloaf

½ pound ground lean beef
1 egg, slightly beaten
⅓ cup soft, fresh bread crumbs
¼ cup shredded Cheddar cheese
3 tablespoons finely chopped onion
2 tablespoons catsup
1 tablespoon finely chopped green pepper
⅛ teaspoon dried thyme leaves
⅛ teaspoon salt
⅛ teaspoon ground black pepper

1. Combine ingredients in a mixing bowl; mix thoroughly.
2. Shape into loaf and place on a microwavable roast rack. Cook covered with waxed paper 4 to 5 minutes at Power Control 10 or until center is no longer pink. Let stand covered 5 minutes.

Makes 2 servings.

Curried Pork Chops

1 can (10¾ ounces) condensed cream of mushroom soup
¼ cup whipping cream
1 medium apple, peeled, cored, and finely chopped
½ cup finely chopped onion
½ cup raisins
2 teaspoons curry powder
¼ teaspoon ground thyme
¼ teaspoon salt
¼ teaspoon ground black pepper
4 pork loin chops, ½ inch thick (1½ to 2 pounds)

1. Combine soup and cream in a mixing bowl. Add remaining ingredients, except pork chops; blend thoroughly.
2. Arrange pork chops in an 8×8×2-inch square glass baking dish. Pour apple mixture over chops. Cover with plastic wrap, vent. Cook 17 to 18 minutes per pound at Power Control 3 or until chops are no longer pink; turn chops over halfway through cooking. Let stand covered 5 minutes.

Makes 4 servings.

Franks in Beer

1 pound frankfurters
1 can (12 ounces) beer
½ cup finely chopped onion

1. Arrange frankfurters in a 2-quart microwavable casserole. Pour beer over frankfurters; sprinkle with onions.
2. Cook covered 6 to 8 minutes at Power Control 10 or until hot. Let stand covered 5 minutes.

Makes 4 servings.

Tropical Ham Kabobs

1 tablespoon butter or margarine
1 tablespoon lemon juice
1 tablespoon packed dark brown sugar
1 tablespoon honey
1 teaspoon soy sauce
½ teaspoon ground ginger
¼ teaspoon ground cloves
½ pound cooked ham, cut into 1-inch cubes
2 medium bananas, cut into 1-inch slices
1 can (8 ounces) pineapple chunks, drained

1. Combine butter, lemon juice, brown sugar, honey, soy sauce, ginger and cloves in a 2-cup glass measuring cup. Cook uncovered 1 to 1½ minutes at Power Control 10 or until brown sugar is melted; stir once.
2. Thread ham, bananas and pineapple alternately on four 9-inch wooden skewers. Arrange kabobs in a 1½-quart microwavable baking dish. Brush with sauce. Cook covered with waxed paper 4½ to 5 minutes at Power Control 10 or until heated through; turn kabobs over and baste with remaining sauce after 2 minutes of cooking.

Makes 4 servings.

Pork Roast with Sauerkraut

1 jar (32 ounces) sauerkraut, drained
1 cup chicken broth
½ cup finely chopped onion
1 teaspoon caraway seeds
½ teaspoon sugar
1 bay leaf
2½ to 3 pound pork shoulder blade roast, boned and tied
1 teaspoon grounded sage
½ teaspoon ground black pepper

1. Combine ingredients, except pork roast, sage and pepper; set aside.
2. Rub roast with sage and pepper. Place roast in cooking bag in an 8×8×2-inch square glass baking dish. Close bag loosely with microwavable closure or string. Cook in bag 22 to 25 minutes per pound at Power Control 3. Turn roast over and add sauerkraut mixture halfway through cooking. Close bag loosely.
3. Cook until internal temperature reaches 165°F. Let stand in bag 15 minutes.

Makes 4 servings.

Veal Paprika

¼ pound boneless veal cutlets, cut into 1½-inch pieces
½ cup sliced fresh mushrooms
¼ cup chicken broth
2 tablespoons finely chopped onion
1 teaspoon paprika
⅛ teaspoon ground thyme
⅛ teaspoon salt
⅛ teaspoon ground black pepper
1 tablespoon dry white wine or dry sherry
2 teaspoons flour
¼ cup dairy sour cream

1. Combine veal, mushrooms, chicken broth, onion, paprika, thyme, salt and pepper in a 1-quart microwavable casserole. Cook covered 3 minutes at Power Control 7; stir once.
2. Blend wine and flour until smooth. Stir into veal mixture. Cook covered 1 to 1½ minutes at Power Control 10 or until sauce is thickened. Stir in sour cream.

Makes 1 serving.

POULTRY

Orange Glazed Duckling

POULTRY

Microwave cooked chicken is juicy and succulent. Whole poultry becomes golden but not crisp. For the crisper, conventional crust, pop the poultry in your conventional oven at 450°F for 10 to 15 minutes after microwaving. The same technique is also convenient when barbecuing. Defrost and precook in your microwave oven then flash-cook on the grill for that barbeque flavor.

Defrosting Poultry: Tips & Techniques

- For best results, remove poultry from its original paper or plastic closed package (wrapper). Otherwise, the wrap will hold steam and juice close to the foods which can cause the outer surface of the foods to cook.
- Place poultry on a microwavable roast rack.
- Defrost only as long as necessary, separating pieces as soon as possible.
- Shield with foil any thin, uneven or warm areas of poultry in the middle of the defrosting cycle.

POULTRY DEFROSTING TABLE

Cut and Weight	Power Control	Time (per pound)	Standing Time	Directions
CHICKEN Chicken Whole (2 to 3 lbs.)	3	6-8 min.	25-30 min.	Turn over once.* Immerse in cold water for standing time.
Cut up (2 to 3 lbs.)	3	5-6 min.	10-15 min.	Turn over once.* Separate pieces when partially thawed.
Breast (Under 4 lbs.)	3	3-5 min.	20 min.	Turn over once.*
Drumsticks (1 to 1½ lbs.)	3	4-6 min.	15-20 min.	Turn over once.* Separate pieces when partially thawed.
CORNISH HENS Whole (1 to 1½ lbs.)	3	5-7 min.	10 min.	Turn over once.*

* Turning, stirring or shielding should be done in the middle of the defrosting cycle.

Cooking Poultry: Tips & Techniques

- Defrost poultry completely before cooking.
- Arrange poultry so that thicker pieces face the outside of the baking dish. If cooking legs, arrange them like spokes of wheels.
- Cover the baking dish with waxed paper to minimize spattering.
- Turn over both whole poultry and poultry pieces to ensure even cooking.
- Drain and discard juices as they accumulate.
- Shield thin or bony pieces with small strips of aluminum foil to prevent overcooking. Keep foil at least one inch from oven walls and other pieces of foil.
- Use a browning agent or cook with a sauce to give browned appearance.
- Cook poultry until no longer pink and juices run clear. Temperatures in thigh meat should be 180°-185°F when done. Let stand covered with foil 10 minutes.

POULTRY COOKING TABLE

Poultry	Power Control	Cooking Time	Special Instructions
CHICKEN			
Breasts, boneless 1 half breast (4-5 oz.) 1 whole breast (10-12 oz.) 2 whole breasts (20-24 oz.)	10	6-6½ minutes per pound 5½-6½ minutes per pound 5-6 minutes per pound	Wash and dry poultry. Remove skin and place breasts, thickest portion to outside, in microwavable baking dish. Brush with butter or browning agent and seasonings if desired. Cover with waxed paper. Cook until no longer pink and juices run clear. Let stand covered 3 minutes.
Cut up fryer (2½-3 lbs.)	10	5-6 minutes per pound	Wash and dry poultry. Place pieces in single layer in microwavable baking dish with thicker pieces to the outside. Brush with butter or browning agent and seasonings if desired. Cover with waxed paper. Cook until no longer pink and juices run clear. Let stand covered 5 minutes.
Whole (3-3½ lbs.)	5	13-14 minutes per pound	Wash and dry poultry. Place breast side down on microwavable roast rack. Brush with butter, or browning agent and seasoning if desired. Cover with waxed paper. Cook ⅓ of estimated time. Turn breast side up, brush on butter, or browning agent. Replace waxed paper. Cook ⅓ of estimated time again. Shield if necessary. Cook remaining ⅓ of estimated time or until no longer pink and juices run clear. Let stand covered with foil 10 minutes. (Temperature may rise about 10°F). Temperature in thigh should be 180°F-185°F when done.
TURKEY			
Breast, boneless (2-3 lbs.)	5	18-20 minutes per pound (165°F)	Place thawed turkey breast on microwavable roast rack. Cover with waxed paper. Cook ⅓ of estimated time. Turn breast over. Replace waxed paper. Cook ⅓ of estimated time again; turn breast over. Shield if necessary. Cook remaining ⅓ of estimated time or until no longer pink and juices run clear. Remove from microwave when desired temperature is reached. Let stand covered with foil 10 minutes. (Temperature may rise about 10°F). Temperature in breast should be 170°F before serving.
Breast, whole (4-9 lbs.)	10 then 5	4 minutes per pound 7-8 minutes per pound (165°F)	Wash and dry poultry. Place turkey breast meat side down on microwavable roast rack. Brush with butter or browning agent and seasonings if desired. Cover with waxed paper. After first cooking time is done turn meat side up. Remove and discard drippings. Brush on butter or browning agent and seasonings if desired. Replace waxed paper. Remove drippings halfway through cooking. Cook until no longer pink and juices run clear. Remove breast from microwave when desired temperature is reached. Let stand covered with foil 10 minutes. (Temperature may rise about 10°F). Temperature in breast should be 170°F before serving.
Drumsticks (1½-2 lbs.)	5	14-16 minutes per pound	Wash and dry poultry. Place pieces with thickest portion to outside on microwavable roast rack. Brush with butter or browning agent and seasonings if desired. Cover with waxed paper. Turn over pieces, shield bone ends with small pieces of foil and replace waxed paper halfway through cooking. Cook until no longer pink and juices run clear. Let stand covered 5 minutes.

POULTRY COOKING TABLE (continued)

Poultry	Power Control	Cooking Time	Special Instructions
Whole (7 to 8 lbs.)	10 then 5	4 minutes per pound then 8-9 minutes per pound	Wash and dry poultry. Place turkey breast side down on microwavable roast rack. Brush with butter or browning agent and seasonings if desired. Cover with waxed paper. Turn breast side up. Brush with butter or browning agent before cooking at PC 5, if desired. Remove and discard drippings 1 or 2 times during second cooking time. Cook until no longer pink and juices run clear. Let stand covered with foil 15 minutes. (Temperature may rise about 10°F). Temperature in breast should be 170°F and temperature in thigh should be 185°F before serving.
CORNISH HENS Whole (1-1½ lbs. each)	10	5-6 minutes per pound (165°F)	Wash and dry poultry. Tie wings to body of hen and the legs to tail. Place hens breast side down on microwavable roast rack. Cover with waxed paper. Turn breast side up halfway through cooking. Shield bone ends of drumsticks with foil. Remove and discard drippings. Brush with butter or browning agent and seasonings if desired. Cook until no longer pink and juices run clear. Remove hens from microwave when desired temperature is reached. Let stand covered with foil 5 minutes. (Temperature may rise about 10°F). Temperature in breast should be 170°F before serving.
DUCKLING (4-5 lbs.)	10 then 5	10 min. 8-10 min. per pound	Wash and dry poultry. Tie legs together and tie wings to body. Place breast side down on microwavable roast rack. Brush with butter or browning agent and seasonings if desired. Cover with waxed paper. Turn breast side up halfway through second cooking time. Shield if necessary. Remove and discard fat 1 or 2 times during cooking. Let stand covered with foil 10 minutes. (Temperature may rise about 10°F). Temperature in breast should be 170°F before serving.

Barbecued Chicken

1½ to 2 pounds chicken pieces, skinned
½ cup barbecue sauce

1. Arrange chicken with thicker pieces to the outside in an 8×8×2-inch square glass baking dish. Cook covered with waxed paper 2 minutes at Power Control 10. Drain and turn chicken over.
2. Brush half of barbecue sauce onto chicken. Cook covered 3 minutes at Power Control 10. Turn chicken over and brush with remaining sauce; cook covered 7 to 8 minutes at Power Control 10 or until juices run clear. Let stand covered 3 minutes.

Makes 2 servings.

Coq au Vin

5 slices bacon, chopped
¼ cup flour
1 can (10¾ ounces) condensed beef broth
1 cup dry red wine
¼ cup chopped green onion
1 to 2 cloves garlic, minced
1 small bay leaf
1 tablespoon tomato paste
1 tablespoon dried parsley flakes
½ teaspoon dried thyme leaves
½ teaspoon salt
¼ teaspoon ground black pepper
2½ to 3 pound chicken, cut into serving size pieces
2 medium carrots, thinly sliced
2 cups sliced fresh mushrooms

1. Place bacon in a 3-quart covered microwavable casserole. Cook covered 4 to 5 minutes at Power Control 10 or until crisp. Blend in flour. Stir in beef broth and wine. Add remaining ingredients, except chicken, carrots and mushrooms; mix well. Add chicken and carrots.
2. Cook covered 12 minutes at Power Control 10; turn chicken over after 8 minutes of cooking. Add mushrooms. Cook covered 10 to 12 minutes at Power Control 7 or until chicken is no longer pink and juices run clear; stir once. Let stand covered 5 minutes.

Makes 4 servings.

Sherried Chicken

2½ to 3 pound chicken, cut into serving pieces, skinned
¼ teaspoon ground black pepper
1 large onion, thinly sliced
⅓ cup dry sherry
1 tablespoon soy sauce
1 tablespoon lemon juice
1 tablespoon flour

1. Arrange chicken with thicker pieces to the outside in an 8×8×2-inch square glass baking dish. Sprinkle with pepper and top with onion. Combine remaining ingredients in a bowl. Pour mixture evenly over chicken. Cover with plastic wrap; even.
2. Cook 14 to 16 minutes at Power Control 10 or until chicken is no longer pink and juices run clear; turn over halfway through cooking. Let stand covered 5 minutes. Stir pan juices until smooth and spoon over chicken.

Makes 4 servings.

Chicken Enchiladas

⅔ cup chopped onion
2 tablespoons oil
1 can (4 ounces) chopped green chilies
¾ cup chopped tomatoes
2 to 3 cloves garlic, minced
½ teaspoon salt
2 cups chopped cooked chicken
8 (6-inch) flour tortillas
1 medium avocado, peeled and pureéd
1 cup shredded Cheddar cheese
1 jar (8 ounces) taco sauce, warmed

1. Combine onion and oil in a 1½-quart microwavable casserole. Cook uncovered 4 to 5 minutes at Power Control 10; stir once. Add chilies, tomatoes, garlic and salt. Cook covered 3 minutes at Power Control 10. Stir in chicken. Cook covered 3 to 4 minutes at Power Control 10 or until chicken is hot.
2. Wrap 4 tortillas in moistened paper towel and cook 1 to 1½ minutes at Power Control 10 or until softened. Spread ¼ cup chicken filling on each tortilla and top with 1 tablespoon of pureéd avocado. Roll tortilla around filling. Repeat with remaining tortillas. Place filled tortillas seam side down in a 1½-quart microwavable baking dish.
3. Cook uncovered 4 to 5 minutes at Power Control 10 or until enchiladas are heated through. Sprinkle enchiladas with cheese. Cook uncovered 1½ to 2 minutes at Power Control 10 or until cheese is melted. Serve with warm taco sauce.

Makes 4 to 8 servings.

Orange Glazed Duckling

¼ cup frozen orange juice concentrate
⅓ cup water or fruit juice
1 beef bouillon cube
1 tablespoon packed dark brown sugar
¼ teaspoon ground black pepper
4 to 5 pound duckling

1. Combine ingredients, except duckling in a 2-cup glass measuring cup. Cook uncovered 2 to 3 minutes at Power Control 10 or until hot; stir twice. Set aside.
2. Remove excess fat from duckling and pierce skin with fork. Tie legs together and tie wings to body. Place breast side down on a microwavable roast rack. Brush with glaze. Cook covered with waxed paper 10 minutes at Power Control 10; drain.
3. Cook covered 8 to 10 minutes per pound at Power Control 5; shield drumsticks during cooking. Brush occasionally with glaze until duckling is no longer pink and juices run clear. Turn over duckling halfway through cooking; drain and discard fat twice. Let stand covered with foil 10 minutes. Discard any remaining glaze.

Makes 4 servings.

Fruited Cornish Game Hen

½ cup diced canned peaches, drained, reserve ¼ cup syrup
½ cup diced canned pears, drained
1 tablespoon lemon juice
1 tablespoon cornstarch
½ teaspoon ground ginger
1 Cornish game hen (about 1½ pounds)

1. Combine peaches, pears, syrup, cornstarch, lemon juice and ginger in a 1-quart glass measuring cup; blend thoroughly. Cook uncovered 2 to 3 minutes at Power Control 10 or until thickened. Cover and set aside.
2. Wash and dry hen. Tie wings to body of hen. Place hen breast-side down on a microwavable roast rack. Cook covered with waxed paper 5 to 6 minutes per pound at Power Control 10. Halfway through cooking time turn hen breast-side up. Shield end of drumsticks with foil. Spoon fruit mixture over hen.
3. Cook uncovered for remaining time until hen is no longer pink and juices run clear. Let stand covered with foil 5 minutes. Temperature in breast should be 170°F. before serving.

Makes 2 servings.

Wine Glazed Turkey Breast

4 to 5 pound bone-in turkey
    breast, thawed
⅓ cup currant jelly
2 tablespoons Madeira, sherry or
    port
¼ teaspoon ground ginger
¼ teaspoon ground thyme
¼ teaspoon salt
⅛ teaspoon ground black pepper

1. Wash turkey breast and pat dry. Place turkey breast meat side up on a microwavable roasting rack. Combine remaining ingredients in a mixing bowl; blend thoroughly. Brush turkey breast with glaze mixture.
2. Cook uncovered 4 minutes per pound at Power Control 10. Turn breast meat side down and brush with glaze. Cook uncovered 8 to 9 minutes per pound at Power Control 5 or until turkey is no longer pink and juices run clear. Turn breast meat-side up and brush with remaining glaze. If areas of the turkey seem to be cooking too quickly, shield them with small pieces of aluminum foil. Let stand, covered with foil 10 minutes. Temperature in breast should be 170°F. before serving. Discard any remaining glaze.

Makes 8 to 10 servings.

Turkey Florentine

1 package (10 ounces) frozen
    chopped spinach, thawed and
    drained
1 cup diced cooked turkey
⅛ teaspoon ground black pepper
1 can (7½ ounces)
    semi-condensed cream of
    mushroom soup
1 tablespoon milk
1 tablespoon dry sherry

1. Spread spinach evenly in bottom of a 1-quart microwavable casserole. Top with turkey and sprinkle with pepper. Blend remaining ingredients in a bowl until smooth. Pour mixture over turkey.
2. Cook covered 6 to 7 minutes at Power Control 10 or until heated through. Let stand covered 2 minutes.

Makes 2 servings.

FISH & SHELLFISH

Fish and shellfish cook beautifully in the microwave. Their naturally high moisture content means fast cooking. In just a few minutes, your seafood will be tender and moist, keeping its true flavor and mild taste.

Defrosting Fish & Shellfish: Tips & Techniques

- For best results, remove fish or seafood from its original paper or plastic closed package (wrapper). Otherwise, the wrap will hold steam and juice close to the food which can cause the outer surface of the foods to cook.
- Place on a microwavable roast rack.
- Shield with foil any thin, uneven or warm areas in the middle of the defrosting cycle.
- To avoid cooking, check at minimum time. Let stand 5 to 10 minutes to complete defrosting.

FISH AND SHELLFISH DEFROSTING TABLE

Cut and Weight	Power Control	Time (per pound)	Standing Time	Directions
FISH Fish fillets 1 lb.	3	4-6 min.	4-5 min.	Defrost in package on dish. Turn over once.* After defrosting, carefully separate fillets under cold water.
Fish steaks 1 lb.	3	4-6 min.	5 min.	Defrost in package on dish. After defrosting, carefully separate steaks under cold running water.
Whole fish 8 to 10 oz. 1½ lb to 2 lbs.	3	4-6 min. 5-7 min.	5 min. 5 min.	Use a shallow dish; the shape of the fish determines size. Cover the head with aluminum foil. Turn over once.* The fish should be icy when removed from oven. Finish thawing while standing at room temperature.
Lobster tails 8 oz. pkg.	3	5-7 min.	5 min.	Remove from package to baking dish.
Crab legs 8 to 10 oz.	3	3-4 min.	5 min.	Use a glass baking dish. Break the legs apart and turn over once.
Crab meat 6 oz.	3	4-5 min.	5 min.	Defrost in package on dish. Break apart and turn over once.
Shrimp 1 lb.	3	3-4 min.	5 min.	Remove from package to dish. Spread loosely in baking dish and rearrange during thawing as necessary.
Scallops 1 lb.	3	6-8 min.	5 min.	Defrost in package. If in block; spread out on baking dish if in pieces. Turn over and rearrange during thawing as necessary.
Oysters 12 oz.	3	3-4 min.	5 min.	Remove from package to dish. Turn over and rearrange during thawing as necessary.

* Turning, stirring or shielding should be done in the middle of the defrosting cycle.

Cooking Fish & Shellfish: Tips & Techniques

- Completely defrost fish and shellfish before cooking.
- Arrange unevenly shaped pieces with thicker parts toward the outside of the dish. Arrange shellfish in a single layer for even cooking.
- Always use the shortest cooking time. Fish is done the moment it turns opaque and the thickest part begins to flake. Shellfish is done when the shell turns from pink to red and the flesh is opaque and firm.
- The type of cover used will determine whether fish is baked or poached. For poached fish cover with microwavable lid or plastic wrap, vented; for baked fish place waxed paper over container.
- Cook fish that is coated or prepared with sauce uncovered or lightly covered with waxed paper. This keeps the coatings from becoming soggy and the sauce from getting watery.

FISH AND SHELLFISH COOKING TABLE

Fish	Power Control	Cooking Time Minutes Per Pound	Special Instructions
Fish fillets	10	5 to 6 minutes	Arrange fish in single layer with thickest portion toward outside edge of 1½-quart microwavable baking dish. Brush with melted butter and season, if desired. Cook covered with plastic wrap; vented. Let stand covered 2 minutes.
Fish steaks	10	5 to 6 minutes	
Whole fish	7	6 to 7 minutes	
Scallops	10	5 to 6 minutes	Prepare as directed above, except stir in place of rotating dish.
Shrimp, shelled	10	5 to 6 minutes	
Lobster tail	10	4 to 5 minutes	Cut hard shell down middle with knife. Grasp tail with both hands and open flat. Place flesh side up in 8×8×2-inch square glass baking dish. Cook covered with waxed paper. Let stand covered 2 minutes.

Poached Fish Fillets

4 orange rough fillets
(1 to 1¼ pound)
½ cup dry white wine
3 tablespoons butter or margarine cut into ¼-inch slices
2 tablespoons finely chopped green onion
¼ teaspoon ground black pepper

1. Arrange fillets with thicker piece to the outside in a 1½-quart microwavable baking dish. Pour wine over fillets. Dot with butter. Sprinkle with onion and pepper.
2. Cook covered with waxed paper 4 to 6 minutes at Power Control 10 or until fish flakes easily when tested with fork. Let stand covered 5 minutes.

Makes 4 servings.

Baked Whitefish Meuniere

½ cup butter or margarine, cut into pieces
¼ cup finely chopped parsley

1 tablespoon lemon juice
1½ to 2½ pounds whole whitefish, cleaned

1. Combine butter, parsley and lemon juice in a 1½-quart microwavable baking dish. Cook uncovered 1 to 2 minutes at Power Control 10 or until butter is melted; stir once.
2. Place fish in baking dish and turn to coat with butter mixture. Cover with plastic wrap; vent. Cook 11 to 12 mintes at Power Control 7 or until fish flakes easily when tested with fork; turn fish over after 5 minutes cooking. Let stand covered 5 minutes.

Makes 3 to 4 servings.

Trout Almondine

¼ cup sliced blanched almonds
2 tablespoons butter or margarine
1 whole trout, cleaned (about 12 ounces)
1 teaspoon lemon juice
⅛ teaspoon salt
⅛ teaspoon ground black pepper

1. Place almonds and butter in a 2-cup glass measuring cup. Cook uncovered 2 to 3 minutes at Power Control 10 or until almonds are lightly toasted; stir twice.
2. Place trout in a 1½-quart microwavable baking dish. Sprinkle with lemon juice, salt and pepper. Top with toasted almonds. Cook covered with waxed paper 3 to 4 minutes at Power Control 10 or until fish flakes easily when tested with fork. Let stand covered 5 minutes.

Makes 1 to 2 servings.

Halibut Divan

1 can (10¾ ounces) condensed cream of shrimp soup
2 teaspoons lemon juice
¼ teaspoon salt
¼ teaspoon ground white pepper
1 pound halibut fillets
1 package (10 ounces) frozen broccoli spears, thawed

1. Combine ingredients, except fillets and broccoli, in a 1-quart glass measuring cup. Cook uncovered 3 to 4 minutes at Power Control 10 or until hot; stir twice. Cover and set aside.
2. Arrange fillets with thicker pieces to the outside in an 8×8×2-inch square glass baking dish. Place broccoli on top of fillets with stalks facing to the outside of dish. Cook covered with waxed paper 8 to 9 minutes at Power Control 10 or until fish flakes easily when tested with fork and broccoli is tender-crisp. Pour sauce over fish and broccoli. Cook covered 2 to 2½ minutes at Power Control 10 or until hot. Let stand covered 3 minutes.

Makes 4 servings.

Seafood Newburg

1 can (10¾ ounces) condensed cream of mushroom soup
¼ cup milk or half-and-half
⅛ teaspoon ground red pepper
⅛ teaspoon ground black pepper
1 package (10 ounces) frozen peas, thawed
1 jar (2½ ounces) mushrooms, drained
2 tablespoons finely chopped onion
1 pound cooked seafood, cut into bite-size pieces
2 to 3 tablespoons sherry

1. Blend soup, milk and peppers in a 2-quart microwavable casserole; mix well. Add peas, mushrooms and onion. Cook covered 4 to 5 minutes at Power Control 10 or until heated through; stir once.
2. Stir seafood and sherry into mushroom mixture. Cook covered 5 to 6 minutes at Power Control 10 or until heated through; stir once. Let stand covered 5 minutes.

Makes 4 servings.

Shrimp Scampi

½ cup butter or margarine
3 to 6 cloves garlic, minced
2 tablespoons lemon juice
1 tablespoon dried parsley flakes
¼ teaspoon salt
¼ teaspoon ground black pepper
1 pound shrimp, shelled and deveined

1. Combine ingredients, except shrimp in an 8×8×2-inch square glass baking dish. Cook uncovered 3 to 4 minutes at Power Control 10 or until butter is melted; stir twice.
2. Stir shrimp into butter sauce. Cover with plastic wrap; vent. Cook covered 4 to 6 minutes at Power Control 10 or until shrimp are opaque. Let stand covered 5 minutes.

Makes 4 servings.

Hot Baked Stuffed Clams

3 slices bacon, chopped
¼ cup finely chopped onion
3 tablespoons olive oil
1 clove garlic, minced
⅔ cup fine dry bread crumbs
2 tablespoons finely chopped parsley
¼ teaspoon ground thyme
¼ teaspoon paprika
¼ teaspoon ground black pepper
Dash ground red pepper
18 small littleneck clams, scrubbed, opened and on the half shell

1. Combine bacon, onion, olive oil and garlic in a 1-quart microwavable casserole. Cook uncovered 3 to 5 minutes at Power Control 10 or until bacon is crisp. Add remaining ingredients, except clams; mix well.
2. Arrange half of clams around the edge of a 10-inch microwavable plate. Pierce each clam several times with wooden pick. Top clams with crumb mixture. Cook covered with waxed paper 3 to 4 minutes at Power Control 5 or until clams are cooked. Repeat with remaining clams.

Makes 3 to 4 servings.

Salmon Quiche

4 eggs
⅔ cup milk
1 can (15½ ounces) canned salmon, drained and cleaned
1 can (4 ounces) sliced mushrooms, drained
2 tablespoons finely chopped green onion
2 tablespoons finely chopped parsley
1 cup shredded Cheddar cheese
⅛ teaspoon ground red pepper
¼ teaspoon salt
1 9-inch baked pastry shell (page 66)

1. Beat eggs and milk together in mixing bowl until blended. Add salmon, breaking up with a fork. Gently stir in remaining ingredients. Pour mixture into baked pastry shell.
2. Cook covered 16 to 18 minutes at Power Control 7 or until center is almost set. Let stand 5 minutes until center becomes firm.

Makes 4 to 6 servings.

Tuna Onion Casserole

2 cans (6½ or 7 ounces) tuna,
undrained
1 can (10¾ ounces) condensed
cream of mushroom soup
1 can (10¾ ounces) condensed
cream of celery soup
2 cups cooked elbow macaroni
1 can (4 ounces) sliced
mushrooms, drained
2 tablespoons lemon juice
½ teaspoon ground black peper
⅛ teaspoon ground thyme
1 can (2.8 ounces) French-fried
onion rings

1. Combine tuna and soups in a 2-quart microwavable casserole.
Stir in remaining ingredients, except onion rings.
2. Cook covered 12 to 15 minutes at Power Control 10 or until hot;
stir twice. Let stand covered 5 minutes. Top with onion rings.

Makes 4 to 6 servings.

VEGETABLES

Green Beans Almondine

VEGETABLES

Vegetables retain their beautiful color, fresh taste and crisp texture when cooked in the microwave oven. Because of their high moisture content, you need only add 2 to 4 tablespoons of water.

Cooking Vegetables: Tips & Techniques

- Pierce the skins of whole potatoes, sweet potatoes and winter squash before cooking. This allows steam to escape and prevents bursting in the oven. When cooking more than one or two whole vegetables arrange in a circle, allowing space in between. Place on paper towel to absorb moisture.
- Fresh vegetables should be cooked in a covered microwavable casserole or baking dish. Add water as directed in the chart.
- Stalk type vegetables like broccoli and asparagus should be arranged with the thicker, tougher portions to the outside of the dish.
- Rearrange large vegetables halfway through cooking to ensure even cooking.
- Frozen vegetables may be cooked in their plastic cooking pouch or original carton after removing the outer wrapping. Vegetables in a carton should be laid on a double thickness of paper towelling to absorb moisture. Cooking pouches should be pierced with a fork to allow steam to escape.
- Most vegetables should be allowed to stand 2 minutes to complete cooking.
- Salt vegetables after cooking. This prevents drying out.
- Lift lid or cover away from you to avoid steam burn.

VEGETABLE COOKING TABLE

Vegetables	Cooking Time Power Control 10	Special Instructions
Artichokes Fresh (8 oz. each) 2 medium 4 medium	6-7 minutes 11-12 minutes	Place trimmed artichokes, right side up, in 8×8-inch microwavable baking dish. Add 2 teaspoons lemon juice and 2 tablespoons water. Cover with plastic wrap and vent. Cook until lower leaves can be pulled off and base pierces easily with fork. Let stand covered 2 minutes.
Frozen, hearts (9 oz. pkg.)	8-9 minutes	Remove outer wrapping from box. Place box on 2 paper towels. Cook until hearts pierce easily with fork. Let stand 2 minutes.
Asparagus, Fresh, spears (1 lb.)	7-8 minutes	Place spears in single layer in 1½-quart microwavable baking dish, alternating tips and thick ends, with thickest stalks to outside of dish. Add 2 tablespoons water. Cover with plastic wrap and vent. Cook until tender-crisp. Let stand covered 2 minutes.
Asparagus, Frozen, spears (10 oz.) Frozen, cut up (10 oz.)	7-8 minutes 5-6 minutes	Remove outer wrapping from box. Place box on 2 paper towels. After cooking let stand 2 minutes.
Beans, green & wax Fresh, cut (1 lb.)	9-10 minutes	Place beans and 2 tablespoons water in 1½-quart microwavable covered casserole. Stir halfway through cooking. Cook until tender-crisp. Let stand covered 2 minutes.
Frozen, (9 oz.)	6-7 minutes	Remove outer wrapping from box. Place box on 2 paper towels. After cooking let stand 2 minutes.
Beans, baby lima Frozen (10 oz.)	5-6 minutes	Remove outer wrapping from box. Place box on 2 paper towels. After cooking let stand 2 minutes.

VEGETABLE COOKING TABLE (continued)

Vegetables	Cooking Time Power Control 10	Special Instructions
Beets, Fresh (1 lb.)	15½-16½ minutes	Place beets and ¼ cup water in 1½-quart microwavable covered casserole. Rearrange halfway through cooking. Cook until beets pierce easily with fork. Let stand covered 2 minutes. Peel after cooking.
Broccoli, Fresh, spears (1 lb.)	6-7 minutes	Place broccoli in single layer in 1½-quart baking dish with flowerets toward center of dish. Add 2 tablespoons water. Cover with plastic wrap and vent. Cook until tender-crisp. Let stand covered 2 minutes.
Frozen, chopped (10 oz.)	7-8 minutes	Remove outer wrapping from box. Place on 2 paper towels. After cooking let stand 2 minutes.
Frozen, spears (10 oz.)	6-7 minutes	
Brussels sprouts Fresh (1 lb.) 3-4 cups	6-7 minutes	Place Brussels sprouts and 2 tablespoons water in 2-quart microwavable covered casserole. Stir halfway through cooking. Cook until tender-crisp. Let stand covered 2 minutes.
Frozen (10 oz.)	6-7 minutes	Remove outer wrapping from box. Place box on 2 paper towels. After cooking let stand 2 minutes.
Cabbage, Fresh, chopped (1 lb.) 1 medium	7-8 minutes	Place cabbage and ¼ cup water in 2-quart microwavable covered casserole. Stir halfway through cooking. Cook until tender-crisp. Let stand covered 2 minutes.
Wedges, (1 lb.) 1 medium	7-8 minutes	Place cabbage and ¼ cup water in 2-quart microwavable covered casserole. Cook until tender-crisp. Let stand covered 2 minutes.
Carrots, Fresh, sliced 2 cups	6-7 minutes	Place carrots and 2 tablespoons water in 1-quart covered casserole. Stir halfway through cooking. Cook until fork-tender. Let stand covered 2 minutes.
Frozen, crinkle cut (10 oz.)	6-7 minutes	Remove outer wrapping from box. Place box on 2 paper towels. After cooking let stand 2 minutes.
Frozen, whole baby (10 oz. pouch)	7-8 minutes	Remove pouch from box. Pierce pouch with fork. Place in 1½-quart microwavable casserole. After cooking let stand 2 minutes.
Cauliflower Fresh, whole (1 lb.)	7-8 minutes	Place trimmed cauliflower and 2 tablespoons water in 1 or 1½-quart covered microwavable casserole. Cook until tender-crisp. Let stand covered 2 minutes.
Fresh, flowerets 2 cups	4-5 minutes	
Frozen, flowerets (10 oz.)	5-6 minutes	Remove outer wrapping from box. Place box on 2 paper towels. After cooking let stand 2 minutes.
Celery, Fresh, sliced, 1 inch pieces 4 cups	8-9 minutes	Place sliced celery and 2 tablespoons water in 1½-quart covered microwavable casserole. Stir halfway through cooking. Cook until tender-crisp. Let stand covered 2 minutes.

VEGETABLE COOKING TABLE (continued)

Vegetables	Cooking Time Power Control 10	Special Instructions
Corn, Fresh, 2 ears	8-10 minutes	Place husked corn and 2 tablespoons water in 1½-quart microwavable baking dish. Cover with plastic wrap and vent. Cook until tender-crisp. Let stand covered 5 minutes.
4 ears	10-12 minutes	
Frozen, 2 ears	6-7 minutes	Place corn in 1½-quart microwavable baking dish. Cover with plastic wrap and vent. Cook until tender-crisp. Let stand covered 5 minutes.
4 ears	11-12 minutes	
Frozen, kernels (10 oz.)	5-6 minutes	Remove outer wrapping from box. Place box on 2 paper towels. After cooking let stand 2 minutes.
Eggplant, Fresh, whole (1 lb.)	5-6 minutes	Pierce eggplant with fork and place on 2 paper towels. Turn over halfway through cooking. Cook until fork pierces skin easily. Let stand 2 minutes. Cut in half to remove pulp.
Fresh, cubed (1 lb.) 5 cups	5-6 minutes	Place eggplant and 2 tablespoons water in 2-quart covered microwavable casserole. Stir halfway through cooking. Let stand covered 2 minutes.
Leeks, Fresh, sliced (8 oz.) 3 cups	6-7 minutes	Place sliced leeks and 2 tablespoon water in 1-quart microwavable covered casserole. Stir halfway through cooking. Let stand covered 2 minutes.
Mixed Vegetables Frozen (10 oz.)	6-7 minutes	Remove outer wrapping from box. Place box on 2 paper towels. After cooking let stand 2 minutes.
Mushrooms, Fresh, sliced (½ lb.)	3-4 minutes	Place sliced mushrooms in 1 to 1½-quart covered microwavable casserole. Stir halfway through cooking. As soon as mushrooms begin to darken, remove and let stand covered 2 minutes.
(1 lb.)	5-6 minutes	
Okra Frozen, whole (10 oz.)	9-10 minutes	Remove outer wrapping from box. Place box on 2 paper towels. After cooking let stand 2 minutes.
Frozen, sliced (16 oz.)	9-10 minutes	Place okra and 2 tablespoons water in 2-quart covered microwavable casserole. Stir halfway through cooking. Let stand covered 2 minutes.
Onions, Fresh, whole pearl (10 oz. pkg.)	6-7 minutes	Place peeled onions and 2 tablespoons water in 1-quart covered microwavable casserole. Stir halfway through cooking. Cook until onions are translucent. Let stand 2 minutes.
Fresh, chopped (8 oz.) 2 medium	5-6 minutes	
Parsnips, Fresh sliced (1 lb.)	6-7 minutes	Place parsnips and 2 tablespoons water in 1½-quart microwavable covered casserole. Stir halfway through cooking. Cook until fork tender. Let stand covered 2 minutes.
Pea pods Frozen (6 oz. pouch)	2½-3½ minutes	Remove pouch from box. Pierce pouch with fork. Place in 1-quart microwavable casserole. After cooking let stand 2 minutes.
Peas and Carrots Fresh (10 oz.)	6-7 minutes	Remove outer wrapping from box. Place box on 2 paper towels. After cooking let stand 2 minutes.

VEGETABLE COOKING TABLE (continued)

Vegetables	Cooking Time Power Control 10	Special Instructions
Peas, black eyed Frozen (16 oz.)	10-11 minutes	Place peas and 2 tablespoons water in 1½-quart covered microwavable casserole. Stir halfway through cooking. Let stand covered 2 minutes.
Peas, green Fresh (1 lb.) 4 cups	8-9 minutes	Place shelled peas and 2 tablespoons water in 1½-quart covered microwavable casserole. Stir halfway through cooking. Let stand covered 2 minutes.
Frozen (9 oz. pouch)	4-5 minutes	Remove outer wrapping from box or pouch. Place box on 2 paper towels. Pierce pouch with fork and place in 1½-quart microwavable casserole. After cooking let stand 2 minutes.
Frozen (10 oz.)	6-7 minutes	
Potatoes, sweet cut up (6-8 oz. each)		Place potatoes and 2 tablespoons water in 1½-quart microwavable covered casserole. Stir halfway through cooking. Let stand covered 2 minutes.
3 medium	7-8 minutes	
whole, (6-8 oz. each) 1 medium potato	3-4 minutes	Pierce potatoes several times with fork. Place in circle on 2 paper towels. Turn over potatoes halfway through cooking. Remove potatoes when soft to the touch. Wrap in foil and let stand 5 minutes.
2 medium potatoes	6-7 minutes	
4 medium potatoes	8-9 minutes	
Potatoes, White cut up (6-8 oz. each) 4 medium	11-12 minutes	Place potatoes and 2 tablespoons water in 1½-quart covered microwavable casserole. Stir halfway through cooking. Let stand covered for 2 minutes.
whole baking (6-8 oz. each) 1 potato	5-6 minutes	Pierce potatoes several times with fork. Place in circle on 2 paper towels. Turn over potatoes halfway through cooking. Remove potatoes when soft to touch. Wrap in foil and let stand 5 minutes.
2 potatoes	7-8 minutes	
4 potatoes	12-13 minutes	
Rutabaga, Fresh, whole (1 lb.)	10-11 minutes	Pierce rutabaga through waxy coating several times with fork. Place on 2 paper towels. Remove halfway through cooking. Cut into quarters, peel and dice. Place diced rutabaga and 2 tablespoons water in 1½-quart microwavable covered casserole. After cooking let stand covered 2 minutes.
Spinach, Fresh, leaf (1 lb.)	6-7 minutes	Place spinach and 2 tablespoons water in 3-quart covered microwavable casserole. After cooking let stand covered 2 minutes.
Frozen, chopped (9 oz. pouch)	5-6 minutes	Remove outer wrapping from box or pouch. Place box on 2 paper towels. Pierce pouch with fork and place in 1½-quart microwavable casserole. After cooking let stand 2 minutes.
(10 oz.)	6-8 minutes	
Frozen, leaf (10 oz.)	7-8 minutes	
Squash, Acorn or Butternut Fresh (1-1½ lbs.) 1 medium	8-9 minutes	Pierce squash several times with fork. Place on 2 paper towels. Carefully remove halfway through cooking. Cut squash in half, remove fibrous strands and seeds. Place in 8×8-inch microwavable baking dish. Cover with plastic wrap and vent. After cooking let stand covered 2 minutes.
Frozen, cooked (12 oz.)	8-9 minutes	Remove outer wrapping from box. Place box on 2 paper towels. After cooking let stand covered 2 minutes.

VEGETABLE COOKING TABLE (continued)

Vegetables	Cooking Time Power Control 10	Special Instructions
Squash, Spaghetti Fresh (2-3 lbs.) 1 medium whole	12-13 minutes	Pierce squash several times with fork. Place squash on 2 paper towels. Turn over several times during cooking. Let stand 2 minutes. Cut in half. Remove fibrous strands and seeds from center.
Succotash, Frozen (10 oz.)	7-8 minutes	Remove outer wrapping from box. Place box on 2 paper towels. After cooking let stand 2 minutes.
Turnips, Fresh (1 lb.)	10-11 minutes	Pierce turnips through waxy coating several times with fork. Place on paper towel. Remove halfway through cooking. Cut into quarters, peel and dice. Place diced turnips and 2 tablespoons water into 1½-quart microwavable covered casserole. After cooking let stand covered 2 minutes.
Zucchini Fresh, sliced (1 lb.) 4 cups	6-8 minutes	Place zucchini and 2 tablespoons water in 1½-quart microwavable covered casserole. Stir halfway through cooking. Let stand covered 2 minutes.
Fresh, whole (1 lb.)	7-8 minutes	Pierce zucchini several times with fork. Place on 2 paper towels. Turn zucchini over and rearrange halfway through cooking. Let stand 2 minutes.
Frozen, sliced (16 oz.)	8-9 minutes	Remove outer wrapping from box. Place box on 2 paper towels. After cooking let stand 2 minutes.

Note: Frozen vegetables in larger or smaller quantity than listed in the chart or those in non-microwavable bags may be cooked approximately 3 to 4 minutes per cup of vegetables. Measure desired amount of vegetables into microwavable covered casserole and cook.

Asparagus Parmesan

2 packages (10 ounces) frozen asparagus
3 tablespoons butter or margarine, cut into small pieces
½ cup grated Parmesan cheese
¼ teaspoon ground black pepper

1. Place asparagus in a 2-quart microwavable casserole. Cook covered 10 to 12 minutes at Power Control 10 or until asparagus is tender; drain well.
2. Gently toss asparagus with butter to coat. Sprinkle with Parmesan cheese and pepper. Cook uncovered 3 minutes at Power Control 7. Let stand 2 minutes.

Makes 4 to 6 servings.

Braised Celery

8 celery ribs, cut into 1-inch lengths
1½ cups sliced fresh mushrooms
½ cup chopped onion
1 can (10¾-ounce) condensed beef broth
2 tablespoons butter
1 tablespoon dried parsley flakes
½ teaspoon whole thyme leaves
¼ teaspoon ground black pepper
2 tablespoons white wine
1 tablespoon cornstarch

1. Place all ingredients, except wine and cornstarch, in a 2-quart microwavable casserole. Cook covered 20 to 22 minutes at Power Control 10 until tender; stir occasionally.
2. Combine wine and cornstarch; stir into celery. Cook uncovered 1 to 2 minutes at Power Control 10 or until sauce thickens; stir once.

Makes 4 servings

Broccoli-Egg Casserole

2 packages (10 ounce) frozen chopped broccoli, thawed and drained
1 can (10¾-ounce) condensed cream of mushroom soup
4 hard-cooked eggs, chopped
¼ cup whipping cream
1 tablespoon sherry (optional)
⅛ teaspoon ground nutmeg
Dash red pepper
¼ teaspoon ground white pepper
½ cup shredded Swiss cheese
⅓ cup fine dry bread crumbs
2 tablespoons butter

1. Combine broccoli and soup in a 2-quart microwavable casserole. Gently stir in eggs, whipping cream, sherry and seasonings. Cook covered 10 to 12 minutes at Power Control 10 or until hot; stir twice.
2. Sprinkle cheese over broccoli; cover. Let stand 3 minutes to melt cheese.
3. Combine bread crumbs and butter in a 1-cup microwavable measuring cup. Cook 1 to 2 minutes at Power Control 10 or until crumbs are lightly browned. Top cheese with toasted crumbs.

Makes 6 to 8 servings.

Creamed Spinach

2 packages (9 ounce) frozen chopped spinach, thawed and drained
2 tablespoon butter
2 tablespoons finely chopped green onion
2 tablespoons flour
1 cup whipping cream
⅛ teaspoon ground nutmeg
½ teaspoon salt
¼ teaspoon ground black pepper

1. Combine spinach, butter and onion in a 1½-quart microwavable casserole. Cook covered 5 minutes at Power Control 10 or until spinach is hot; stir twice.
2. Blend flour into spinach. Stir in remaining ingredients. Cook uncovered 4 to 5 minutes at Power Control 7 or until mixture thickens; stir twice. Let stand covered 2 mintues.

Makes 4 to 6 servings.

Green Beans Almondine

2 tablespoons slivered almonds
2 tablespoons butter or margarine
½ pound fresh green beans, cut
2 tablespoons water
½ teaspoon lemon juice
¼ teaspoon salt
⅛ teaspoon ground black pepper

1. Combine almonds and butter in a 1-cup glass measuring cup. Cook uncovered 1½ to 2½ minutes at Power Control 10 or until almonds are lightly toasted; set aside.
2. Combine green beans and water in a 1-quart microwavable casserole. Cook covered 5 to 6 minutes at Power Control 10 or until tender-crisp; drain. Toss green beans with toasted almonds and remaining ingredients.

Makes 2 servings.

Mashed Potatoes

2 pounds potatoes, peeled and quartered
3 tablespoons water
¾ cup milk
¼ cup butter or margarine
½ teaspoon salt
¼ teaspoon ground white pepper

1. Place potatoes and water in a 3-quart microwavable casserole. Cook covered 9 to 11 minutes at Power Control 10 or until potatoes are tender; stir twice. Let stand covered 5 minutes; drain. Beat with electric mixer until smooth.
2. Combine remaining ingredients in a 2-cup glass measuring cup. Cook uncovered 1½ to 2 minutes at Power Control 10 or until butter is melted and mixture is hot. Gradually beat milk mixture into potatoes until smooth. To reheat mashed potatoes, cook covered 2 to 3 minutes at Power Control 10 or until heated thoroughly.

Makes 6 servings.

Mustard-Topped Cauliflower

1 medium cauliflower
2 tablespoons water
½ cup mayonnaise
1 tablespoon finely chopped onion
2 teaspoons prepared mustard
¼ teaspoon salt
⅔ cup shredded Cheddar or Swiss cheese
¼ teaspoon paprika (optional)

1. Place cauliflower in a 3-quart microwavable casserole; add water. Cook covered 7 to 8 minutes at Power Control 10 or until cauliflower is tender; drain.
2. Combine remaining ingredients, except cheese and paprika. Spoon mixture over cauliflower; sprinkle with cheese and paprika. Cook uncovered 2 to 3 minutes at Power Control 7 or until cheese is melted. Let stand 1 minute.

Makes 6 servings.

Rich Stuffed Baked Potatoes

1 medium baking potato
1 tablespoon butter or margarine
1 tablespoon milk or half-and-half
1 tablespoon crumbled bacon or snipped chives (optional)
1 tablespoon shredded Swiss cheese
1 tablespoon grated Parmesan cheese
⅛ teaspoon salt
⅛ teaspoon ground black pepper

1. Pierce potato with a fork and place on 2 paper towels in oven. Cook uncovered 5 to 6 minutes at Power Control 10 or until soft to the touch; turn over halfway through cooking. Let stand 5 minutes.
2. Cut potato in half, scoop out cooked potato and combine with butter in a mixing bowl. Add milk and mash lightly; the potato should remain somewhat lumpy. Stir in remaining ingredients. Fill potato shell with mashed potatoes and place on a microwavable serving dish. Cook uncovered 2 to 2½ minutes at Power Control 7 or until heated through. Let stand 1 minute.

Makes 1 serving.

Zucchini Casserole

6 slices bacon, separated
1 cup chopped onion
4 medium zucchini, cut into ½-inch slices
1 cup tomato sauce or pizza sauce
1 clove garlic, minced
½ teaspoon oregano
½ teaspoon salt
¼ teaspoon ground black pepper
1 cup shredded mozzarella cheese

1. Place bacon in a 2-quart microwavable casserole. Cook covered with a paper towel 6 to 6½ minutes at Power Control 10 or until crisp. Remove bacon and crumble. Pour off all but 2 tablespoons bacon drippings. Add onions and garlic to drippings. Cook uncovered 4 to 5 minutes at Power Control 10 or until tender; stir twice.
2. Stir in remaining ingredients, except cheese. Cook covered 8 to 9 minutes at Power Control 10 or until zucchini is tender; stir twice.
3. Sprinkle zucchini with mozzarella cheese; cover. Let stand 3 minutes.

Makes 6 to 8 servings.

Lasagna

PASTA, RICE & CEREAL

Microwave cooking and conventional cooking of pasta, rice and cereal take about the same amount of time. But the convenience of cooking in the serving dish gives the microwave oven the edge. There is no stirring needed and leftover pasta tastes just like fresh cooked when reheated in the microwave oven.

Cooking Pasta, Rice & Cereal: Tips & Techniques
• When using rice or pasta casserole, undercook so it is still firm.
• Allow for stand time with rice and cereal; pasta needs no stand time.

PASTA COOKING TABLE

Type of Pasta	Power Control	Cooking Time	Special Instructions
Spaghetti 4 cups water	10	11½ to 12½ minutes	Combine hot tap water and salt, if desired. Use a ½-quart microwavable baking dish and cover with plastic wrap, vented, for spaghetti and lasagna noodles. Use 3-quart microwavable casserole and cover with microwavable lid or plastic wrap, vented, for macaroni and egg noodles. Cook at Power Control 10 as directed in chart or until water boils. Stir in pasta; cook covered at Power Control 6 as directed in chart or until tender. Drain in a colander.
Add 8 oz. spaghetti	6	10 to 11 minutes	
Macaroni 3 cups water	10	9 to 10 minutes	
Add 2 cups macaroni	6	6 to 7 minutes	
Lasagna noodles 4 cups water	10	12 to 13 minutes	
Add 8 oz. lasagna noodles	6	13 to 14 minutes	
Egg noodles 6 cups water	10	17½ to 18½ minutes	
Add 4 cups noodles	6	6 to 7 minutes	

RICE COOKING TABLE

Type of Rice	Power Control	Cooking Time	Special Instructions
Long grain 2¼ cups water	10	4 to 5 minutes	Combine hot tap water and salt, if desired, in 2-quart microwavable casserole. Cover with microwavable lid or plastic wrap, vented. Cook as directed in chart at Power Control 10 or until water boils. Stir in rice and any seasonings. Cook covered as directed in chart at Power Control 6 or until water is absorbed and rice is tender. Let stand covered 5 to 10 minutes. Fluff with fork.
Add 1 cup rice	6	15 minutes	
Brown 2½ cups water	10	5 to 6 minutes	
Add 1 cup water	6	34 minutes	
Long grain and wild rice mix 2⅓ cups water	10	4½ to 5½ minutes	
Add 6 oz. pkg.	6	25 minutes	
Quick cooking 1 cup water	10	2 to 3 minutes	Follow directions above for boiling water. Stir rice into boiling water and let stand, covered 5 to 10 minutes or until water is absorbed and rice is tender. Fluff with fork.
Add 1 cup rice	not required		

Rice Pilaf

1 cup long grain rice
6 tablespoons butter or margarine
¼ cup finely chopped onion
¼ cup finely chopped celery
2¼ cups chicken broth
1 small bay leaf
⅛ teaspoon ground thyme
¼ teaspoon salt
¼ teaspoon ground black pepper

1. Combine rice and butter in a 2-quart microwavable casserole. Cook uncovered 5½ to 6½ minutes at Power Control 10 or until rice begins to brown; stir every minute. Add onion and celery. Cook uncovered 2 to 3 minutes at Power Control 10 or until vegetables are tender; stir in remaining ingredients.
2. Cook covered 20 to 21 minutes at Power Control 6; stir twice during cooking. Let stand covered 5 minutes.

Makes 4 to 6 servings.

Fettucine Alfredo

½ cup butter or margarine, cut into pieces
½ cup whipping cream
½ pound medium egg noodles, cooked according to chart (page 50)
1 cup grated Parmesan cheese
¼ teaspoon ground black pepper

1. Combine butter and cream in a 1½-quart glass measuring cup. Cook uncovered 1 to 2 minutes at Power Control 10 or until butter melts; stir twice.
2. Stir hot noodles into butter mixture; toss. Add Parmesan cheese and pepper; toss again.

Makes 4 servings.

Noodles Florentine

2 cups shredded Swiss cheese
2 cups sour cream
1 package (10 ounces) frozen chopped spinach, thawed and drained
½ pound medium egg noodles, cooked according to chart (page 50)
½ cup whipping cream
⅓ cup finely chopped green onion
½ teaspoon salt
¼ teaspoon ground black pepper
⅛ teaspoon ground nutmeg

1. Combine ingredients in a 2-quart microwavable casserole; blend well.
2. Cook covered 13 to 14 minutes at Power Control 7 or until heated through; stir twice. Let stand covered 3 minutes.

Makes 6 servings.

Macaroni and Cheese

½ pound uncooked elbow
    macaroni
2 cups hot water
3 tablespoons butter or margarine
½ cup finely chopped onion
¼ teaspoon salt
¼ teaspoon ground black pepper
2¼ cups milk
12 ounces cheese, cut into cubes
    (about 3 cups)
⅓ cup flour

1. Combine macaroni, water, butter, onion, salt and pepper in 3-quart microwavable casserole. Cook covered 6 minutes at Power Control 10 and then 5 minutes at Power Control 5 or until water is absorbed; stir twice.
2. Stir in remaining ingredients. Cook covered 20 to 25 minutes at Power Control 6 or until macaroni is tender and sauce is thickened; stir twice. Let stand covered 5 minutes. Stir.

Makes 4 servings.

Lasagna

1 pound lean ground beef
½ pound sausage meat
1 can (28 ounce) tomato sauce
1 can (4 ounce) sliced
    mushrooms, drained
2 teaspoons dried oregano or
    basil leaves
1 clove garlic, minced
½ teaspoon ground black pepper
9 lasagna noodles (6 ounces),
    cooked according to chart
    (page 50)
1 cup ricotta cheese
1 package (6 ounces) sliced
    mozzarella cheese
⅔ cup grated Parmesan cheese

1. Crumble beef and sausage into a microwavable sieve or colander. Place colander into a 1½-quart microwavable casserole, to collect drippings. Cook covered with waxed paper 5 to 6 minutes at Power Control 10 or until no longer pink; stir twice. Drain fat. Place meat in casserole. Stir in tomato sauce, mushrooms, oregano, garlic and pepper.
2. Cut noodles to fit baking dish. Spread 1 cup of sauce on bottom of a 1½-quart microwavable baking dish; layer ⅓ of the noodles, ⅓ of remaining sauce, ½ of the ricotta cheese and ½ of the mozzarella cheese. Add a second layer of ⅓ of the noodles, ⅓ of the sauce and the remainder of the ricotta cheese and mozzarella cheese. Layer with the last ⅓ of the noodles and sauce. Sprinkle with Parmesan cheese. Cook covered with waxed paper 25 to 27 minutes at Power Control 8 or until lasagna is hot in the center. Let stand covered 10 minutes.

Makes 6 servings.

Fruity Oatmeal

⅔ cup hot water
⅓ cup quick-cooking oats
1 tablespoon chopped dried
    apricots or raisins
1 tablespoon packed dark brown
    sugar
⅛ teaspoon salt
1 teaspoon butter
¼ teaspoon ground cinnamon
Dash ground nutmeg
Dash ground ginger
Dash ground cloves or allspice

1. Bring water to boil in a 1½-quart microwavable casserole. Add oats, apricots, sugar and salt; mix thoroughly. Cook covered 1 to 1½ minutes at Power Control 10 or until thickens; stir twice.
2. Add remaining ingredients; stir to blend. Let stand covered 1 minute.

Makes 1 serving.

EGGS & CHEESE

Spinach Ring with Cheese

EGGS & CHEESE

Basic Scrambled Eggs

Eggs	Tablespoons of Milk	Teaspoons of Butter	Cooking time Power Control 8	Special Instructions
1	1	1	50 to 60 seconds	Use 10-ounce microwavable bowl or custard cup for 1 to 2 eggs; use 1-quart microwavable casserole for 4 to 6 eggs. Place butter in dish. Cook uncovered 20 to 40 seconds at Power Control 10 or until butter melts. Beat eggs and milk together with fork until well blended; stir into melted butter. Cook uncovered as directed in chart at Power Control 8. Break up and stir eggs with fork halfway through cooking. Cover with waxed paper and let stand 1 to 3 minutes. Stir and season to taste.
2	2	2	2 to 2½ minutes	
4	4	4	3½ to 4 minutes	
6	6	6	4½ to 5½ minutes	

Basic Omelet

1 tablespoon butter or margarine
2 eggs
2 tablespoons milk
⅛ teaspoon salt
Dash of ground black pepper

1. Place butter in a 9-inch glass pie plate. Cook uncovered 15 to 20 seconds at Power Control 10 or until melted. Tilt plate to cover bottom with melted butter.
2. Beat eggs, milk, salt and pepper in small bowl. Pour mixture into pie plate. Cook covered 2 to 3 minutes at Power Control 8 or until almost set; stir after 1 minute. Cover with plastic wrap and let stand 2 minutes.

Makes 1 to 2 servings.

Eggs Benedict

1 package (⅛ ounce) Hollandaise sauce mix, prepared and heated according to package directions
4 eggs, poached
2 English muffins, split and toasted
4 thin slices cooked ham

1. Prepare Hollandaise sauce, poached eggs and English muffins; set aside and keep warm. Place ham slices in a single layer on a microwavable dinner plate. Cook 1 to 1½ minutes at Power Control 10 or until heated through.
2. Place English muffin halves on a microwavable plate. Cover each with a slice of ham and top with a poached egg. Spoon sauce on top. Reheat by cooking uncovered 3 to 4 minutes at Power Control 8.

Makes 4 servings.

Ranchero Eggs

¼ cup finely chopped green
    pepper
¼ cup finely chopped onion
2 tablespoons butter or margarine
1 clove garlic, minced
1 can (28 ounces) tomatoes,
    drained and chopped
1 can (3 ounces) chilies, drained
    and mashed
½ teaspoon salt
½ teaspoon ground black pepper
6 eggs
1 cup shredded Monterey Jack or
    Cheddar cheese

1. Combine green pepper, onion, butter and garlic in a 2-quart microwavable casserole. Cook uncovered 3 to 4 minutes at Power Control 10 or until vegetables are tender-crisp; stir twice. Add tomatoes, chilies, salt and pepper. Cook covered 5 minutes at Power Control 10; stir once.
2. Slip eggs on top of tomato mixture along the edge of dish. Pierce each yolk with wooden pick. Cook covered 4 to 5 minutes at Power Control 8 or until eggs are almost set. Sprinkle with cheese. Let stand covered 2 minutes.

Makes 4 to 6 servings.

Welsh Rarebit

2 tablespoons butter or margarine
2 tablespoons flour
¼ teaspoon dry mustard
¼ teaspoon Worcestershire sauce
Dash red pepper
Dash ground nutmeg
¼ teaspoon salt
Dash ground black pepper
½ cup milk
¼ cup beer
1 cup shredded Cheddar cheese
    toast, biscuits or toasted English
    muffins

1. Place butter in a 1-quart glass measuring cup. Cook 30 to 45 seconds at Power Control 10 or until melted. Stir in flour and seasonings; blend to make a smooth paste. Gradually add milk; stir until smooth. Cook uncovered about 1½ to 2 minutes at Power Control 10 or until thickened; stir after 1 minute.
2. Gradually stir beer into milk mixture; add cheese. Cook 1 to 1½ minutes at Power Control 7 or until cheese is melted; stir twice. Serve over toast, biscuits or toasted English muffins.

Makes 2 servings.

Spinach Ring with Cheese

2 packages (9 ounces) frozen
    chopped spinach, thawed and
    drained
1 cup cottage cheese
½ cup shredded Swiss cheese
¼ cup grated Parmesan cheese
2 eggs
⅛ teaspoon ground thyme
½ teaspoon salt
¼ teaspoon ground black pepper
¼ cup cracker crumbs (optional)

1. Combine ingredients, except cracker crumbs in a mixing bowl; blend thoroughly. Pour mixture into a buttered microwavable 10 to 12-cup tube dish; cover with waxed paper.
2. Cook 11 to 12 minutes at Power Control 7 or until set. Let stand covered 5 minutes. Invert onto serving platter. Sprinkle with cracker crumbs.

Makes 6 to 8 servings.

SANDWICHES

Pizza Rolls

SANDWICHES

Who doesn't like a sandwich? As a snack, lunch or light supper, only one thing can enhance its appeal. Heating it! It takes just seconds in the microwave oven and it's so easy.

Heating Sandwiches: Tips & Techniques
- Sandwiches heat very quickly because they are porous.
- Wrap sandwiches in a paper towel or napkin and place on a microwavable roast rack to prevent the bread from getting soggy.
- Cook the sandwich until it feels warm, not hot. Overheating causes the bread to become tough and dry.
- Reheat fillings like sloppy joes separately. Add to heated roll and serve.

Pizza Rolls

½ pound ground lean beef
2 tablespoons finely chopped onion
¼ teaspoon garlic powder
¼ cup tomato sauce or pizza sauce
¼ teaspoon dried basil or oregano leaves
¼ teaspoon salt
⅛ teaspoon ground black pepper
1 Italian roll (about 6 inches long)
⅓ cup shredded mozzarella cheese

1. Crumble beef and place in a microwavable sieve or colander; add onion and garlic powder. Place sieve in 1½-quart microwavable casserole to collect drippings. Cook covered with waxed paper 2 to 2½ minutes at Power Control 10 or until no longer pink; drain fat. Place meat in casserole. Stir in tomato sauce, basil, salt and pepper.
2. Split roll in half lengthwise and place on a microwavable roast rack.
3. Spoon beef mixture evenly over each roll half and sprinkle with cheese. Cook uncovered 3 to 4 minutes at Power Control 6 or until cheese is melted and rolls are hot.

Makes 2 servings.

Cheeseburgers

1 pound ground lean beef
4 slices American process cheese
4 hamburger buns

1. Shape ground beef into four 4-inch patties. Arrange on a microwavable roast rack. Cover with waxed paper and cook 3 to 4½ minutes at Power Control 10 or until desired doneness; turn patties over halfway through cooking; drain liquid.
2. Top patties with cheese. Cook 30 seconds at Power Control 7. Let stand 2 minutes. Serve on hamburger buns.

Makes 4 servings.

Beef and Tomato Pitas

1 cup plain yogurt
½ cup chopped green pepper
2 tablespoons finely chopped onion
¼ teaspoon dried mint leaves
1½ pounds ground lean beef
1 clove garlic, minced
1 can (8 ounces) stewed tomatoes, chopped
1 tablespoon dried parsley flakes
4 loaves (6-inch) pita bread
1½ cups shredded lettuce

1. Combine yogurt, green pepper, onion and mint in a bowl to make dressing; set aside.
2. Combine ground beef and garlic in a 2-quart microwavable casserole. Cook covered with waxed paper 4 to 5 minutes at Power Control 10 or until no longer pink; stir twice. Drain. Stir in tomatoes and parsley. Cook covered 2 to 2½ minutes at Power Control 10 or until heated thoroughly; stir once.
3. Spoon beef mixture evenly over each pita bread and sprinkle with shredded lettuce. Serve with yogurt dressing.

Makes 4 servings.

Reuben Sandwiches

8 slices dark rye or pumpernickel bread, toasted
½ pound cooked corned beef, sliced
1 can (8 ounces) sauerkraut, rinsed and drained
½ cup creamy Russian or Thousand Island dressing
4 slices Swiss cheese

1. Layer corned beef, sauerkraut and dressing on 4 bread slices. Top each with cheese and remaining bread slices. Wrap each sandwich with a paper towel and place on a microwavable roast rack.
2. Cook 4 to 5 minutes at Power Control 6 or until sandwich is heated through.

Makes 4 servings.

Ham and Egg Sandwiches

¼ cup finely chopped onion
¼ cup finely chopped green pepper
3 tablespoons butter or margarine
4 eggs, lightly beaten
1 small tomato, seeded, chopped and drained
⅔ cup cubed cooked ham
4 hamburger or hard rolls

1. Combine onion, green pepper and butter in an 8-inch round glass cake dish. Cook uncovered 4½ to 5½ minutes at Power Control 10.
2. Add remaining ingredients, except rolls, to baking dish. Cook uncovered 5 to 6 minutes at Power Control 8 or until almost set; break up and stir eggs once, halfway through cooking. Let stand 2 minutes. Cut into 4 wedges and place in split rolls.

Makes 4 servings.

BREADS

Cooking Bread: Tips & Techniques

- Microwaved breads and muffins have greater volume than those conventionally baked. Fill loaf dish or muffin cups about half full to avoid spilling over when cooking.
- To give breads or muffins a browner, more 'baked' appearance, add spices such as cinnamon to the batter or toppings of chopped nuts, toasted coconut, or cinnamon and sugar.
- Always underestimate cooking times. Breads will continue to bake during stand time. Under cooking is a good practice in reheating too.
- Breads, which are very porous, overcook quickly and become tough.
- Microwave cooked breads are moister in appearance than their conventional counterparts.
- Muffins are done when a toothpick inserted into the center comes out clean. They will appear barely set and may have a couple of moist spots on top, which will disappear after standing.

Apricot Walnut Bread

¼ cup milk
½ cup water
1 cup chopped dried apricots
2 tablespoons grated orange peel (one medium orange)
¾ cup packed dark brown sugar
1 egg, slightly beaten
3 tablespoons vegetable oil
1½ cups flour
1 teaspoon baking powder
¼ teaspoon ground nutmeg or mace
½ teaspoon salt
¾ cup chopped walnuts

1. Combine milk, water, dried apricots and orange peel in a 2-quart glass measuring cup. Cook uncovered 2 to 3 minutes at Power Control 10 or until mixture begins to bubble around the edge.
2. Add brown sugar, egg and oil to fruit mixture; blend thoroughly. Combine flour, baking powder, nutmeg and salt in a mixing bowl; stir to blend. Add to fruit mixture; stir only until dry ingredients are moistened. Stir in nuts. Pour batter into a waxed paper-lined 9×5×3-inch microwavable loaf dish.
3. Cook uncovered 9 to 10 minutes at Power Control 7; shield corners with foil halfway through cooking. When done, top will appear moist and wooden pick inserted near center will come out clean. Let stand covered with waxed paper on a flat surface 5 minutes. Remove from dish and peel off waxed paper. Cool on rack.

Makes 1 loaf.

Banana Bread

2 cups buttermilk baking mix
½ cup packed dark brown sugar
3 tablespoons flour
¼ teaspoon ground nutmeg or mace
¼ cup milk
1 egg, slightly beaten
⅔ cup mashed banana
⅔ cup chopped dates
⅔ cup chopped walnuts

1. Combine baking mix, brown sugar, flour and nutmeg in a mixing bowl, stir to blend. Combine milk, egg and banana in a mixing bowl and add to dry mixture; stir only until dry ingredients are moistened. Stir in dates and nuts. Pour batter into a waxed paper-lined 9×5×3-inch microwavable loaf dish.
2. Cook 10½ to 11½ minutes at Power Control 7; shield corners with foil halfway through cooking. When done, top will appear moist and wooden pick inserted near center will come out clean. Let stand covered with waxed paper on a flat surface for 5 minutes. Remove from dish and peel off waxed paper. Cool on rack.

Makes 1 loaf.

Garlic Bread

¼ cup (½ stick) butter
½ teaspoon garlic powder
⅛ teaspoon salt
⅛ teaspoon ground black pepper
1 loaf (6-inch) French bread, cut ⅔ of the way through at 1-inch intervals

1. Combine butter, garlic, salt and pepper in a 2-cup glass measuring cup. Cook uncovered 45 to 60 seconds at Power Control 2 or until butter is softened but not melted; beat to blend.
2. Spread butter mixture between slices in bread. Wrap loaf loosely in waxed paper for a soft loaf or place unwrapped on a paper towel for a crisper loaf. Cook 1 minute at Power Control 10 or until hot.

Makes 1 loaf.

Orange Raisin Bread

3 cups flour
3 tablespoons sugar
1 teaspoon baking powder
½ teaspoon salt
3 tablespoons butter or margarine
1 cup buttermilk
1 egg
1 tablespoon grated orange peel
1 tablespoon baking soda
1½ cups raisins
1 tablespoon caraway seeds

1. Combine flour, sugar, baking powder and salt in a mixing bowl; cut in butter.
2. Combine buttermilk, egg, orange peel and baking soda in a small bowl. Stir mixture into dry ingredients; mix only until dry ingredients are moistened. Stir in raisins and caraway seeds.
3. On a lightly floured surface, shape dough into an 18×3-inch roll. Shape roll into a ring on a buttered 10-inch microwavable plate.
4. Cook uncovered 9 to 10 minutes at Power Control 7 or until bread is firm. Let stand 15 minutes. Serve warm.

Makes 1 loaf.

Pumpkin Bread

1 cup canned pumpkin
2 eggs
1 teaspoon vanilla extract
1 cup chopped walnuts or pecans
½ cup vegetable oil
⅓ cup water
½ teaspoon ground cinnamon
½ teaspoon ground cloves or mace
1½ cups sugar
1¼ cups flour
1 teaspoon baking soda
½ teaspoon salt

1. Combine pumpkin, eggs, vanilla, nuts, oil, water and spices in a mixing bowl; stir in sugar. Combine flour, baking soda and salt in a separate bowl; stir into pumpkin mixture. Blend until ingredients are moistened. Pour batter into a waxed paper lined 9×5×3-inch glass loaf dish.
2. Cook uncovered 16 to 18 minutes at Power Control 7; shield corners with foil halfway through cooking. When done, top will appear moist and a wooden pick inserted near center will come out clean. Let stand covered with waxed paper on a flat surface 5 minutes. Remove from dish and remove waxed paper. Cool on rack.

Makes 1 loaf.

Sticky Buns

2 tablespoons butter or margarine
2 tablespoons packed dark brown sugar
2 tablespoons chopped pecans or walnuts
¼ teaspoon ground cinnamon
⅓ cup buttermilk baking mix
2 tablespoons cold water
1 teaspoon grated orange peel

1. Place 1 tablespoon butter in each of two 6-ounce custard cups. Cook uncovered 45 to 60 seconds at Power Control 10 or until melted. Swirl custard cups to coat sides with butter. Add 1 tablespoon each brown sugar and chopped nuts to each cup. Sprinkle with cinnamon. Return to oven and cook uncovered 45 to 60 seconds at Power Control 10 or until hot and bubbly; Stir.
2. Blend remaining ingredients in a mixing bowl until smooth. Divide batter evenly into custard cups. Cook uncovered 1½ to 2 minutes at Power Control 10 or until top springs back when pressed with a finger. Immediately invert custard cups onto a serving platter. Let stand covered with custard cups 2 minutes.

Makes 2 buns.

Orange Coffee Cake Ring

1 cup finely chopped walnuts or pecans, divided
3 tablespoons packed dark brown sugar
1½ teaspoons ground cinnamon
½ cup orange juice
¼ cup sugar
1 egg
2 cups buttermilk baking mix
½ cup orange marmalade

1. Combine ½ cup walnuts, brown sugar and cinnamon in a mixing bowl. Sprinkle mixture in a paper towel lined 10-cup microwavable fluted tube dish.
2. Combine orange juice, sugar and egg in a bowl. Stir in baking mix; blend well. Add remaining ½ cup walnuts and marmalade; stir only until dry ingredients are moistened. Pour batter into prepared dish.
3. Cook covered with paper towel 10 to 11 minutes at Power Control 7 or until wooden pick inserted comes out clean. Let stand covered 5 minutes. Invert onto serving plate.

Bran Muffins

⅓ cup milk
1 egg
¼ cup whole bran cereal
¼ cup vegetable oil
¼ cup raisins
¼ cup molasses
¾ cup flour
1 teaspoon baking powder
¼ teaspoon baking soda
¼ teaspoon ground cinnamon
⅛ teaspoon salt

1. Beat milk and egg together in a mixing bowl; stir in bran cereal and let stand 1 minute. Stir in oil, raisins and molasses. Add flour, baking powder, baking soda, cinnamon and salt; stir only until dry ingredients are moistened. Place 2 paper liners in each microwavable muffin ring cup. Fill each cup two-thirds full (about 3 tablespoons).
2. Cook uncovered 3½ to 4 minutes at Power Control 7. Remove muffins to a rack. Let stand 2 minutes.

Makes 6 muffins.

Corn Muffins

½ cup flour
½ cup yellow corn meal
2 tablespoons sugar
2 teaspoons baking powder
¼ teaspoon baking soda
¼ teaspoon salt
1 egg, slightly beaten
½ cup milk or buttermilk
3 tablespoons vegetable oil or melted butter

1. Combine flour, corn meal, sugar, baking powder, baking soda and salt in a mixing bowl. Add egg, milk and oil; stir until ingredients are moistened. Place 2 paper liners in each microwavable muffin ring cup. Fill each cup two-thirds full (about 3 tablespoons).
2. Cook uncovered 3 to 3½ minutes at Power Control 7. Remove muffins to a rack. Let stand 2 minutes.

Makes 6 muffins.

Pineapple Muffins

⅓ cup packed dark brown sugar
3 tablespoons butter or margarine, softened
1 egg
1 can (8 ounces) crushed pineapple in syrup, drained, reserve ¼ cup syrup
1 cup flour
1 teaspoon baking powder
½ teaspoon salt
½ cup chopped pecans or walnuts

1. Cream brown sugar and butter in a mixing bowl. Beat in egg, pineapple and reserved syrup. Add flour, baking powder, salt and pecans; stir only until dry ingredients are moistened. Place 2 paper liners in each cup of a microwavable muffin ring. Fill each paper liner two-thirds full with batter (about 3 tablespoons).
2. Cook uncovered 3½ to 4 minutes at Power Control 7 or until wooden pick inserted near center comes out clean and tops of muffins appear slightly moist. Let stand 2 minutes. Remove muffins to rack. Repeat with remaining batter.

Makes 12 muffins.

CAKES & PIES

Make your very next cake or pie in the microwave. Not only do they cook in half the time, but they are delicious! Cakes are superior in texture, height and lightness to conventional ones. Pie crust comes out extra flaky.

Microwave Cakes & Pies: Tips & Techniques

- When making pie fillings, slightly reduce the amount of liquid given in the conventional recipe.
- Pastry will not brown, but it does come out extra flaky. To add color, brush prepared shell with vanilla extract before cooking.
- All pies should be cooked in a microwavable pie plate. Prick pastry before cooking. To check doneness, the bottom of the crust should look opaque and dry.
- Crumb crusts work well in the microwave.
- Because microwave cooked cakes rise much higher than those conventionally baked, fill dish only half full.
- Cakes are done when a toothpick inserted near the center of the layer comes out clean. There may be some moist spots on top immediately after removing from the oven. These will disappear during the stand time.
- Angel food cake, chiffon cake and cream puffs need dry heat so bake in a conventional oven for best results.

CONVENIENCE CAKES AND MIXES COOKING TABLE

Cakes & Mixes	Power Control	Cooking Time	Special Instructions
Brownie Mix (23.6 oz.)	7	12-14 minutes	Prepare as directed on package. Spread batter into greased 8×8×2-inch square glass baking dish. Shield corners with foil halfway through cooking. When done, top will appear puffy and dry and will spring back when lightly pressed with finger. Let stand covered with waxed paper on flat surface 10 minutes. Remove waxed paper. Cool before cutting.
Cake, layer (17-18½ oz.)	7	5-6 minutes	Prepare as directed on package. Divide batter between two paper towel-lined 8-inch microwavable cake dishes. Fill each dish half full. Any extra batter may be used for cupcakes. Cover with paper towel. When done, wooden pick inserted near center will come out clean. Let stand covered on flat surface 5 minutes. Invert onto serving plate. Carefully remove paper towel. Repeat with second layer.
Cake, tube (17-18½ oz.)	7	11-13 minutes	Prepare as directed on package. Pour batter into paper towel-lined 10- to 12-cup microwavable fluted tube dish. Cover with paper towel. When done, wooden pick inserted near center will come out clean. Let stand covered on flat surface 10 minutes. Invert onto serving plate. Cool.

CONVENIENCE CAKES AND MIXES COOKING TABLE (continued)

Cakes & Mixes	Power Control	Cooking Time	Special Instructions
Cup Cakes			Prepare as directed on package. Place 2 paper liners in each microwavable muffin ring cup. Fill each cup two-thirds full with batter (about 3 tablespoons). When done, tops will appear moist and wooden pick inserted near center will come out clean. Let stand 2 minutes. Remove cupcakes to rack. Repeat with remaining batter.
4 cup cakes	7	1½-2 minutes	
6 cup cakes	7	2-3 minutes	
Date Bread Mix (17 oz.)	7	11-12 minutes	Prepare as directed on package. Pour batter into waxed paper-lined 9×5×3-inch microwavable loaf dish. Shield corners with foil halfway through cooking. When done, top will appear moist and wooden pick inserted near center will come out clean. Let stand covered with waxed paper on flat surface 5 minutes. Remove from dish and carefully peel off waxed paper. Cool on rack.
Muffins (13 oz.)	7	3-3½ minutes	Prepare as directed on package. Place 2 paper liners in each microwavable muffin ring cup. Fill each cup two-thirds full with batter (about 3 tablespoons). When done, tops will appear moist and wooden pick inserted near center will come out clean. Let stand 2 minutes. Remove muffins to rack. Repeat with remaining batter.

Fruitcake

1 cup chopped dried apricots
1 cup raisins or dried currants
1 cup slivered almonds
¾ cup candied cherries, halved
¾ cup candied pineapple
¾ cup flour
¾ cup packed dark brown sugar
½ cup shortening
3 eggs
2 tablespoons rum or brandy
2 teaspoons vanilla extract
¼ teaspoon almond extract
½ teaspoon ground nutmeg or mace
½ teaspoon baking powder
½ teaspoon salt

1. Line a 10 to 12-cup microwavable tube dish with paper towels; set aside.
2. Combine ingredients in a mixing bowl; blend thoroughly. Pour batter into prepared pan. Cook covered with paper towel 13 to 14 minutes at Power Control 7 or until cake pulls away from the sides of the pan. Let stand 15 minutes on a flat surface before inverting onto a rack to cool. To store, wrap in foil or plastic wrap and refrigerate no longer than 4 weeks.

Makes 1 cake.

Apple-Nut Upside Down Cake

3 tablespoons butter
⅓ cup firmly packed brown sugar
¼ cup chopped walnuts
1 teaspoon pumpkin pie spice
1 medium cooking apple, peeled, cored and sliced
1 package (9 ounces) yellow cake mix

1. Place butter in 8-inch round glass cake dish. Cook 30 to 45 seconds at Power Control 10 or until butter melts; stir in brown sugar, walnuts and pumpkin pie spice. Spread evenly over bottom of dish. Arrange apple slices in overlapping pinwheel design. Cook 2 to 3 minutes at Power Control 10 or until apple slices are tender. Set aside.
2. Prepare cake mix according to package directions. Pour batter over apples. Cook covered with paper towel 5 to 6 minutes at Power Control 7 or until wooden pick inserted near center comes out clean.
3. Let stand covered on a flat surface 5 minutes. Invert onto serving plate.

Makes 6 servings.

Coconut Cake

1 package (18½ ounces) yellow cake mix
1 package (3½ ounces) coconut flavored instant pudding mix
4 eggs
1 cup water
¼ cup vegetable oil
1 jar (12 ounces) strawberry or raspberry preserves
1 container (8 ounces) frozen dessert topping, thawed
1½ cups flaked coconut

1. Combine cake mix, pudding mix, eggs, water and oil in a mixing bowl. Beat at medium speed for 4 minutes. Pour batter into a paper towel lined 10 to 12-cup microwavable tube dish. Cook covered with paper towel 13 to 14 minutes at Power Control 7 or until wooden pick inserted near center comes out clean. Let stand covered on a flat surface for 5 minutes. Invert onto serving plate; remove paper towel. Let stand until cool.
2. Split cake horizontally into 3 layers. Spread with preserves and reassemble. Frost with dessert topping and sprinkle with coconut. Store covered in the refrigerator.

Makes 1 cake.

Devil's Food Cake

¾ cup sugar
¼ cup butter or margarine, softened
1 egg
½ teaspoon vanilla extract
⅔ cup water
1 cup flour
¼ cup cocoa
¾ teaspoon baking soda
½ teaspoon salt

1. Cream together sugar and butter in a mixing bowl; add egg and vanilla beating until fluffy. Blend in water. Beat in remaining ingredients until thoroughly mixed. Pour batter into paper towel-lined 8-inch round glass cake dish.
2. Cook covered with paper towel 7½ to 8½ minutes at Power Control 7. When done, wooden pick inserted near center comes out clean. Let stand covered on flat surface 5 minutes. Invert onto serving plate, remove paper towel.

Makes 1 layer.

Peachy Cheesecake

1 can (16 ounces) peach halves, drained
1 package (8 ounces) cream cheese, softened
⅓ cup sugar
2 eggs
1 tablespoon lemon juice
¼ teaspoon vanilla extract
1 graham cracker crust (page 66)

1. Pureé peaches in blender or food processor. Add remaining ingredients, except pie crust; blend until smooth.
2. Pour mixture into crust. Cook uncovered 17 to 19 minutes at Power Control 7 or until center is almost set. Cool. Chill 3 hours or overnight.

Plain Pastry Shell

1 cup flour
½ teaspoon salt
6 tablespoons butter or margarine, chilled and cut into ¼-inch slices
3 to 4 tablespoons ice water

1. Combine flour and salt in mixing bowl. Add butter slices and cut into flour. Add water 1 tablespoon at a time; stir with a fork to gather dough. Form into a ball.
2. Place dough on lightly floured work surface. Roll out ⅛-inch thick (about a 12-inch circle) and place in a 9-inch glass pie plate. Trim and flute edge. Prick the sides and bottom of the shell thoroughly with a fork.
3. Cook uncovered 11 to 12 minutes at Power Control 7 or until pastry looks dry and flaky. Cool on flat surface before filling.

Makes 1 9-inch shell.

Cookie or Graham Cracker Crumbs Shell

6 tablespoon butter or margarine
1½ cups graham cracker or cookie crumbs (vanilla wafers, chocolate wafers, or ginger snaps)

1. Place butter in a 9-inch glass pie plate. Cook uncovered 45 to 60 seconds at Power Control 10 or until melted; stir in crumbs. Press mixture against bottom and sides of pie plate to form crust.
2. Cook uncovered 1½ to 2 minutes at Power Control 10 or until firm. Cool before filling.

Makes 1 9-inch crust.

Cherry Cordial Pie

3 cups miniature marshmallows
½ cup milk
½ cup maraschino cherries, drained and chopped
¼ cup cherry liqueur
1 cup whipping cream, whipped
1 9-inch baked chocolate cookie crumb crust
Whipped cream
Maraschino cherries halves

1. Combine marshmallows and milk in a 2-quart microwavable casserole. Cook uncovered 1½ to 2 minutes at Power Control 10 or until marshmallows melt and puff; stir until smooth. Add chopped cherries and liqueur; blend thoroughly. Cool to room temperature, about 30 minutes.
2. Fold whipped cream into marshmallow mixture and spoon filling into prepared crumb crust. Refrigerate 4 hours. Garnish with whipped cream and maraschino cherry halves.

Makes 1 pie.

Peach Pie

2 boxes (16 ounces each) frozen peaches, thawed
⅓ cup sugar
2 tablespoons lemon juice
3 tablespoons cornstarch
⅛ teaspoon ground cinnamon
⅛ teaspoon ground nutmeg
1 9-inch baked pastry shell
Whipped cream
Ice cream

1. Combine peaches, sugar, lemon juice, cornstarch, cinnamon and nutmeg in 2-quart glass measuring cup; stir. Cover with plastic wrap; vent.
2. Cook 11 to 13 minutes at Power Control 10 or until peaches are tender and filling thickens; stir twice. Pour into prepared pastry shell. Serve warm with whipped cream or ice cream

Makes 1 pie.

PUDDINGS, CUSTARDS, & FRUIT DESSERTS

Rich Chocolate Mousse

PUDDINGS, CUSTARDS & FRUIT DESSERTS

Puddings, custards and sophisticated fruit desserts can be made in just a few minutes in the microwave. On the range top you must stir custards and puddings constantly to keep them free from lumps and scorching. Microwaving makes creamy, smooth desserts with minimum attention. Fruit desserts keep their shape, texture and taste.

Cooking Puddings, Custards & Fruit Desserts: Tips & Techniques

- Mix puddings and custards right in the microwavable cooking container. Since they are milk-based be sure the container is large enough to prevent "boil-overs". The same container can be used for serving.
- Do not overcook puddings or custards. Overcooking causes it to curdle.
- After cooking pudding, cover the top with plastic wrap to prevent a "skin" from forming during cooling.

Creamy Vanilla Pudding

½ cup sugar
2 tablespoons cornstarch
⅛ teaspoon salt
2 cups milk
1 egg, well beaten
2 tablespoons butter or margarine
2 teaspoons vanilla extract

1. Combine sugar, cornstarch and salt in a 1½-quart microwavable casserole. Gradually add milk; stir until smooth. Cook uncovered 5 to 7 minutes at Power Control 7 or until thickened; stir twice.
2. In a separate bowl, beat egg with ⅔ cup of the hot pudding mixture. Stir warm egg mixture into bowl with remaining pudding. Cook uncovered 2 to 3 minutes at Power Control 7 or until mixture thickens; stir every minute. Add butter and vanilla; stir until butter melts. Refrigerate.

Makes 4 servings.

Egg Custard

¾ cup milk
2 eggs
2 tablespoons sugar
2 tablespoons grated lemon peel
½ teaspoon vanilla extract
Pinch of salt
Ground nutmeg

1. Pour milk into a 2-cup glass measuring cup. Cook 1 to 1½ minutes at Power Control 7 or until almost boiling. Beat eggs slightly in a mixing bowl; add remaining ingredients except nutmeg. Stir milk into egg mixture.
2. Pour custard mixture into two buttered 6-ounce custard cups. Place cups in oven. Cook uncovered 4 to 5 minutes at Power Control 5 or until set. Remove cups and sprinkle with nutmeg. Set on rack to cool.

Makes 2 servings.

Rich Chocolate Mousse

¾ cup sugar, divided
1 envelope plain gelatin
3 eggs, separated
1 cup milk
3 (1-ounce) squares unsweetened baking chocolate, melted
1 cup whipping cream

1. Combine ½ cup sugar and gelatin in a 2-quart microwavable casserole; beat in egg yolks and milk. Cook uncovered 4 to 5 minutes at Power Control 7 or until mixture thickens slightly and begins to steam; stir every 2 minutes. Beat in chocolate. Refrigerate until mixture holds it shape; stir occasionally.
2. In a glass or metal mixing bowl, beat egg whites until soft peaks form. Sprinkle on remaining ¼ cup sugar and continue to beat until whites are stiff. Beat whipping cream until stiff. Fold first the whites then the whipped cream into the chilled chocolate mixture. Spoon into a small souffle dish. Refrigerate for 4 hours or until firm.

Makes 8 servings.

Fruit Compote

1 cup pitted prunes
1 can (8½ ounces) apricot halves, undrained
1 can (8½ ounces) sliced pears, undrained
1 cup sliced peeled apples
1 tablespoon lemon juice
1 tablespoon dark rum or brandy (optional)
¼ teaspoon ground cinnamon
¼ teaspoon ground cloves

1. Combine ingredients in a 1½-quart microwavable casserole. Cook covered 8 to 10 minutes at Power Control 10 or until apples are tender; stir 3 times. Serve warm or chilled.

.Makes 4 to 6 servings.

Pineapple Bread Pudding

¼ cup butter or margarine
1 package (3½ ounces) instant vanilla pudding
1 teaspoon cinnamon
3 eggs, slightly beaten
3 cups milk
1 can (8¼ ounces) crushed pineapple, undrained
½ cup flaked coconut
1 teaspoon rum extract (optional)
8 slices white bread, French bread or raisin-nut bread, cut into ½-inch cubes
1 tablespoon cinnamon-sugar

1. Melt butter in a 2-quart glass measuring cup 45 seconds at Power Control 10. Add pudding mix, cinnamon, eggs, milk, undrained pineapple, coconut and rum extract; blend thoroughly.
2. Fold in bread cubes. Pour mixture into an 8×8×2-inch square glass baking dish. Sprinkle with cinnamon-sugar. Cook uncovered 25 to 27 minutes at Power Control 8 or until knife inserted near center comes out clean. Let stand on a flat surface for 10 minutes. Serve warm.

Makes 12 servings.

BAR COOKIES & CANDIES

Best-Ever Almond Bark

BAR COOKIES & CANDIES

Homemade bar cookies and candies have always been a special favorite. But now you can make them more often and not spend all day doing it. Even old-fashioned candies like fudge and peanut brittle work well in the microwave.

Cooking Bar Cookies & Candies: Tips & Techniques

- Shield the corners of bar cookies with foil halfway through cooking to avoid overcooking.
- Fudge-like brownies remain moist inside; test cake-like bars with wooden pick.
- When cooking candy, use a container that can withstand high temperatures and will hold two or three times the volume of the ingredients.
- Use conventional candy thermometer only when the candy is out of the oven. Candy thermometers specially designed for microwave use are available and can be used in the oven while cooking.

Best-Ever Almond Bark

¼ pound white chocolate, chopped
¼ cup raisins
¼ cup whole unblanched almonds

1. Place chocolate in a 1-quart glass measuring cup. Cook uncovered 1½ to 2 minutes at Power Control 7 or until melted; stir twice. Stir in raisins and almonds.
2. Pour mixture in a thin layer onto waxed paper; cool thoroughly. Break into pieces.

Makes about ⅓ pound.

Butter Scotch Krispie Treats

½ cup butterscotch pieces
2 tablespoons butter or margarine
2½ cups miniature marshmallows
2½ cups crisp rice cereal

1. Combine butterscotch pieces and butter in a 2-quart microwavable glass casserole. Cook uncovered 2 to 3 minutes at Power Control 7 or until melted. Stir in marshmallows. Cook uncovered 2 to 3 minutes at Power Control 7 or until marshmallows are softened; stir twice. Blend until smooth.
2. Stir rice cereal into marshmallow mixture. Press into buttered 8×8×2-inch square glass baking dish. Let stand until cool and set. Cut into squares.

Makes about 25 squares.

Peanut Brittle

2 cups sugar
1 cup light corn syrup
½ cup water
2 cups shelled peanuts, unsalted
2 tablespoons butter or margarine
2 teaspoons vanilla extract
2 teaspoons baking soda
½ teaspoon salt

1. Combine sugar, corn syrup and water in a 2-quart glass measuring cup. Cook uncovered 8 minutes at Power Control 10.
2. Stir peanuts and butter into mixture. Cook uncovered 17 to 18 minutes at Power Control 10 or until mixture forms threads when dropped in cold water or measures 300°F on a candy thermometer. (Oven should not be in operation when candy thermometer is inserted.) Stir 4 to 5 times during cooking.
3. Stir in remaining ingredients; blend until smooth. Pour mixture onto two buttered baking sheets. Spread in thin layer with a knife. Let stand until hard, about ½ hour. Break into pieces.

Makes about 2 pounds candy.

Caramel Apples

1 package (14 ounces) caramel candy, unwrapped
1 tablespoon water
2 teaspoons butter or margarine, softened
¾ cup chopped nuts
6 small apples
Wooden sticks

1. Combine candy and water in a 1-quart glass measuring cup. Cook uncovered 3 to 4 minutes at Power Control 7 or until melted and smooth; stir every minute.
2. Spread softened butter on a sheet of waxed paper 18-inches long. Sprinkle waxed paper with nuts. Insert stick into each apple. Dip apples into melted caramel turning to coat then roll in nuts. Let stand 10 minutes to harden.

Makes 6 apples.

Chocolate Chip Bars

½ cup butter or margarine
¾ cup packed brown sugar
2 eggs, lightly beaten
1 teaspoon vanilla extract
1 cup chopped nuts
1 package (6 ounces) semisweet chocolate chips
1½ cups flour
1 teaspoon baking powder
Confectioner's sugar

1. Place butter in a 2-quart glass measuring cup. Cook uncovered 30 to 45 seconds at Power Control 10 or until melted. Add brown sugar, eggs and vanilla extract; blend well. Add nuts, chocolate chips, flour and baking powder; mix thoroughly. Spread batter in a greased 8×8×2-inch square glass baking dish.
2. Cook uncovered 7 to 8 minutes at Power Control 7 or until wooden pick inserted near center comes out clean; shield corners with foil halfway through cooking. Cool thoroughly in baking dish. Sprinkle with confectioner's sugar. Cut into bars.

Makes 25 bars.

Applesauce Fudge Squares

½ cup butter or margarine
2 (1 ounce) squares unsweetened chocolate
1 cup packed dark brown sugar
½ cup applesauce
2 eggs
2 teaspoons vanilla extract
1 cup flour
½ teaspoon baking powder
¼ teaspoon baking soda
1 cup chopped walnuts

1. Place butter and chocolate in a 2-quart glass measuring cup. Cook uncovered 2 to 2½ minutes at Power Control 10 or until melted. Stir in brown sugar, applesauce, eggs and vanilla extract. Blend in flour ¼ cup at a time. Add baking powder and soda. Stir in nuts. Pour batter into a greased 1½-quart microwavable baking dish.
2. Cook uncovered 7 to 8 minutes at Power Control 7 or until wooden pick inserted near center comes out clean; shield corners with foil halfway through cooking. Let stand covered with waxed paper 10 minutes. Remove waxed paper; cool thoroughly in baking dish. Cut into squares. Store in tightly covered container.

Makes 16 squares.

BEVERAGES

Spicy Hot Chocolate

BEVERAGES

It is convenient to mix and heat beverages right in the same cup. Instant coffee, tea, cider and bouillon will heat in just a few minutes. Even coffee purists will love the microwave. Brew a full pot, turn it off and reheat later in the microwave for a fresh-brewed flavor.

Heating Beverages: Tips & Techniques

- When heating more than one cup or mug, arrange in a circle, allowing space between each for more even heating.
- You can microwave beverages in styrofoam cups — even china can be used as long as it has no metallic decoration.
- Room temperature liquids will reheat faster than refrigerated beverages.
- Milk tends to boil over in the microwave oven. It's a good practice to heat in a container about twice the size of the milk mixture.
- Stir all heated beverages to distribute heat evenly.

Spicy Hot Chocolate

2 cups milk, divided
¼ cup sugar
1½ (1 ounce) squares unsweetened chocolate
½ teaspoon ground cinnamon
⅛ teaspoon ground nutmeg
⅛ teaspoon ground cloves
Whipped cream
Ground cinnamon

1. Place ½ cup milk, sugar, chocolate, cinnamon, nutmeg and cloves in a 1-quart glass measuring cup. Cook uncovered 3½ to 4 minutes at Power Control 8 or until chocolate melts; stir twice. Mix until smooth.
2. Gradually blend in remaining milk. Cook uncovered 3 to 3½ minutes at Power Control 8 or until hot; stir twice. Pour into cups and garnish with whipped cream and sprinkle with cinnamon.

Makes about 2 cups.

Irish Coffee

¾ cup water
1 rounded teaspoon instant coffee granules
2 teaspoons sugar
2 tablespoons Irish whiskey
Whipped cream

1. Combine water, instant coffee and sugar in an 8-ounce micro-wavable coffee cup. Cook uncovered 1 to 1½ minutes at Power Control 10 or until hot.
2. Stir in whiskey and garnish with whipped cream.

Makes about 1 cup.

Orange Coffee

4 cups water
3 tablespoons instant coffee granules
¾ cup orange liqueur
½ cup whipped cream
2 tablespoons confectioner's sugar
Grated peel of 1 orange

1. Combine water and instant coffee in a 2-quart glass measuring cup. Cook uncovered 8 to 9 minutes at Power Control 10 or until hot; stir once. Stir in orange liqueur.
2. Combine whipped cream and confectioner's sugar. Pour coffee into cups and garnish with sweetened whipped cream; sprinkle with orange peel.

Makes 4 cups.

English Wassail

4 cups apple cider
½ cup lemon juice
½ cup packed dark brown sugar
1 teaspoon whole cloves
½ teaspoon whole allspice
⅛ teaspoon ground nutmeg or mace

1. Combine ingredients in a 2-quart glass measuring cup.
2. Cook uncovered 11 to 12 minutes at Power Control 10 or until mixture boils. Strain before serving.

Makes 5 cups.

Hot Apricot Cocktail

3 cups apricot nectar
½ cup lemon juice
¼ cup packed dark brown sugar
2 cinnamon sticks, broken
1 teaspoon whole cloves

1. Combine ingredients in a 2-quart glass measuring cup.
2. Cook uncovered 7 to 8 minutes at Power Control 10 or until hot; stir once. Let stand 5 minutes. Strain before serving.

Makes about 4 cups.

Coffee-Orange Liqueur

2 cups vodka
1½ cups orange juice
1 tablespoon vanilla extract
1⅔ cups sugar
⅓ cup instant coffee granules

1. Combine ingredients in a 2-quart glass measuring cup; stir until coffee is dissolved. Cook uncovered 8 to 9 minutes at Power Control 10 or until hot; stir once.
2. Cool; cover with plastic wrap and refrigerate overnight.

Makes about 4½ cups.

Strawberry Liqueur

1½ pints strawberries, hulled
2 cups sugar
2 cups vodka

1. Place strawberries in a 2-quart glass measuring cup and crush lightly with a spoon. Stir in sugar and vodka. Cook uncovered 25 minutes at Power Control 5; stir twice.
2. Let stand covered 3 to 4 days. Strain before serving.

Makes about 2 cups.

APPENDIX

REHEATING TABLE

To heat or reheat successfully in the microwave, it is important to follow several guidelines. Measure the amount of food in order to determine the time needed to reheat. Arrange the food in a circular pattern for best results. Room temperature food will heat faster than refrigerated food. Canned foods should be taken out of the can and placed in a microwavable container. The food will heat more evenly if covered with a microwavable lid or plastic wrap, vented. Remove cover carefully to prevent steam burns. Use the following chart as a guide for reheating cooked food.

Item	Power Control	Cook Time	Special Instructions
Sliced meat 3 slices (¼-inch thick)	8	1 to 1½ minutes	Place sliced meat on microwavable plate. Cover with plastic wrap; vent. * Note: gravy or sauce helps to keep meat juicy.
Chicken pieces 1 breast 1 leg and thigh	8 8	2 to 2½ minutes 1½ to 2 minutes	Place chicken pieces on microwavable plate. Cover with plastic wrap; vent.
Fish fillet (6-8 oz.)	8	1½ to 2 minutes	Place fish on microwavable plate. Cover with plastic wrap; vent.
Lasagna 1 serving (10½ oz.)	8	4 to 5 minutes	Place lasagna on microwavable plate. Cover with plastic wrap; vent.
Casserole 1 cup 4 cups	8 8	1½ to 2 minutes 5 to 6 minutes	Cook covered in microwavable casserole; stir once halfway through cooking.
Casserole, cream or cheese 1 cup 4 cups	5 5	3 to 3½ minutes 12 to 13 minutes	Cook covered in microwavable casserole; stir once halfway through cooking.
Sloppy joe or barbecued beef 1 sandwich (½ cup meat filling without bun)	9	50 to 60 seconds	Reheat filling and bun separately. Cook filling covered in microwavable casserole; stir once. Heat bun as directed in chart below.
Mashed potatoes 1 cup 4 cups	8 8	2 to 3 minutes 6½ to 7 minutes	Cook covered in microwavable casserole; stir once halfway through cooking.
Baked beans 1 cup	9	2 to 2½ minutes	Cook covered in microwavable casserole; stir once halfway through cooking.
Ravioli or pasta in sauce 1 cup 4 cups	9 9	2 to 3 minutes 8 to 9 minutes	Cook covered in microwavable casserole; stir once halfway through cooking.
Rice 1 cup 4 cups	9 9	1 to 1½ minutes 4 to 5 minutes	Cook covered in microwavable casserole; stir once halfway through cooking.
Sandwich roll or bun 1 roll	8	15 to 20 seconds	Wrap in paper towel and place on roast rack.
Vegetables 1 cup 4 cups	9 9	1 to 2 minutes 6 to 7 minutes	Cook covered in microwavable casserole; stir once halfway through cooking.

INDEX

Printed in Korea